# THE ESSENTIAL RESILIENCE & WELLBEING TOOLKIT

## EARLY YEARS & YOUNGER CHILDREN

# THE ESSENTIAL RESILIENCE & WELLBEING TOOLKIT FOR EARLY YEARS & YOUNGER CHILDREN

Activities & Strategies for Professionals & Parents

HINTON HOUSE Early Years Resources

HINTONHOUSE

First published in 2019 by

**Hinton House Publishers Ltd**
**T** +44 (0)1280 822557 **E** info@hintonpublishers.com

**www.hintonpublishers.com**



**British Library Cataloguing in Publication Data**
A CIP catalogue record for this book is available from the British Library.

ISBN 978 1 906531 28 7

Printed and bound in the United Kingdom

# Contents

## Part 2 Activities



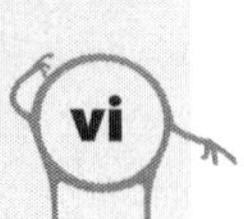

## Part 3 Handouts for Parents, Carers & Professionals



## Part 4 Recommended Reading & Resources

# List of Worksheets

# About the Authors

**Dr Tina Rae** has more thirty years' experience working with children, adults and families in both clinical and educational contexts within local authorities and specialist educational services. She currently works as a consultant educational and child psychologist in a range of SEMH and mainstream contexts and for Compass Fostering as a consultant psychologist supporting foster carers, social workers and looked-after children. From 2010 to 2016 she was an academic and professional tutor for the Doctorate in Educational and Child Psychology at the University of East London. Tina is a registered member of the Health and Care Professions Council and a full member of the British Psychological Society. She is also a member of ENSEC (European Network for Social and Emotional Competence) and a former trustee of the Nurture Group Network (NGN) now NurtureUK.

Tina has published more than 100 titles on topics including wellbeing, attachment, emotional literacy, behavioural problems, anger and stress management, critical incidents, cognitive behavioural therapy, motivational interviewing, solution-focused brief therapy, loss and bereavement in young people, youth offending and social skills development.

Among her most recent publications are *The Essential Guide to Using CBT with Children & Young People* (2018), *Identifying & Supporting Children with Sensory Processing Difficulties* (2018), *Understanding & Preventing Self-Harm in Schools* (2017), *The Essential Guide to Using Mindfulness with Children & Young People* (2017), all from Hinton House Publishers.

Tina is a regular speaker at both national and international conferences and events and also provides training courses and supervision for school-based staff in both special and mainstream contexts and educational psychology services across the UK and internationally.

tinarae@hotmail.co.uk

**Dr Jo Wood** is an educational psychologist working in an outer London local education authority. Her doctoral research was on the use of 'Solution Circles' to structure supervision for school staff.

Before beginning her training as an educational psychologist, Jo was a secondary school science teacher in London for many years. She was also a head of science, teacher training fieldwork tutor, teaching assistant and tutor. Jo's last teaching job was three years as Head of Science in a pupil referral unit in an inner London borough.

Jo is co-author with Tina Rae of *The Essential Guide to Using Mindfulness with Children & Young People* (2017), from Hinton House Publishers.

# Introduction

> It is difficult to make people miserable when they feel worthy of themselves.
>
> — *Abraham Lincoln*

This comprehensive resource bank is a 'must have' for all early years practitioners and those who support young children in a range of contexts – teachers, social workers, parents, carers, nurture practitioners and nursery staff.

At this time of significant focus and concern about the mental health needs of young people in Britain (as evidenced by the 'Heads Together' campaign – www.headstogether.org.uk – led by the Duke and Duchess of Cambridge), practical resources that empower teachers, parents and other professionals to create effective responses are very welcome. This is particularly so when the focus is on prevention in the early years, as opposed to remediation once problems have become entrenched.

The key to supporting the mental wellbeing of younger children is to focus on building resilience at the earliest opportunity, via meaningful engagement in a range of evidence-based strategies and approaches. Emphasising the importance of a resilient staff team and a whole-school approach based on the philosophy and approaches of Positive Psychology is also a key objective for all of us who work with children and young people.

This book therefore aims to support staff, parents and carers in meeting these objectives. It makes use of a range of key tools and strategies from evidence-based approaches, such as mindfulness, solution-focused brief therapy and cognitive behavioural therapy. These are the tools that enable children and young people to develop the resilience they will need to cope with the challenges of life in both the learning and social context.

Interest in the area of resilience first developed in the early 1970s, issuing from research that aimed to identify the factors placing young people at risk of developing various problems, such as drug abuse, delinquency or mental disorders.

Researchers noticed that many young people who had been exposed to numerous 'risk factors' nevertheless developed into healthy, competent adults. These researchers became interested in studying the resilience of these young people and turned their attention to identifying the 'protective factors' – both internal and external – that help a person to bounce back from, or thrive in spite of, adverse circumstances. These protective factors have now been identified in some detail, providing a clear picture of what makes some people more resilient than others.

## Risk versus Resilience

The resilience approach, which emphasises individuals' strengths and resources, is often contrasted with the risk-based approaches from which it originally developed (Garmezy, 1991). Whilst it is true that their emphases are different, in fact both approaches are complementary and necessary. Identifying risks is only of benefit to the extent that we are able to either reduce those risks, or help individuals to cope in spite of them. On the other hand, programmes that aim to promote resilience will be more effective if they target 'at risk' individuals, for the obvious reason that those who are coping with adversity have greater need to be resilient than those whose lives are relatively easy.

One of the criticisms levelled against the risk-based approach is that it highlights deficits, rather than strengths. In doing so, it creates the possibility of negative stereotyping and stigmatisation. It can also trigger the 'self-fulfilling prophecy' effect, whereby young people who are identified as 'at risk' are treated differently and regarded as less able than their peers. It is well established that low expectations may actually *cause* poor performance, thereby reinforcing those low expectations and creating a vicious circle. On the other hand, resilience research has clearly shown that high expectations tend to have the opposite effect, creating a cycle of positive reinforcement that can be highly beneficial (Benard, 1991).

Whilst assessment of risk continues to be important, the resilience movement has emphasised the importance of prioritising the development of each person's individual strengths and their natural capacity for successful adaptation.

## An Ecological Approach

There is a universal human tendency to over-estimate the importance of internal, personality factors and under-estimate the impact of the environment in explaining the behaviour of individuals. This has been referred to as the 'fundamental attribution error'. In the context of resilience, this error manifests as a tendency to see any child's ability to function effectively or poorly as a reflection of their 'nature', rather than their context or circumstances. However, resilience research has increasingly embraced an ecological model, in which the child's functioning and behaviour is viewed within the context of a web of bi-directional relationships, including family, school, peers, neighbourhood and the wider society.

Whilst genetic factors do play a role in resilience, ultimately much more important is the quality of inter-personal relationships and the availability of networks of support. Programmes that target the cognitive underpinnings of resilience – optimism, self-esteem, autonomy, and so forth – are important. However, the ecological perspective (Bronfenbrenner, 1979) suggests that treating children as isolated units of cognitive functioning is a limited approach. Ultimately resilience is not an attribute of any single individual; it is an attribute of communities, schools and families.

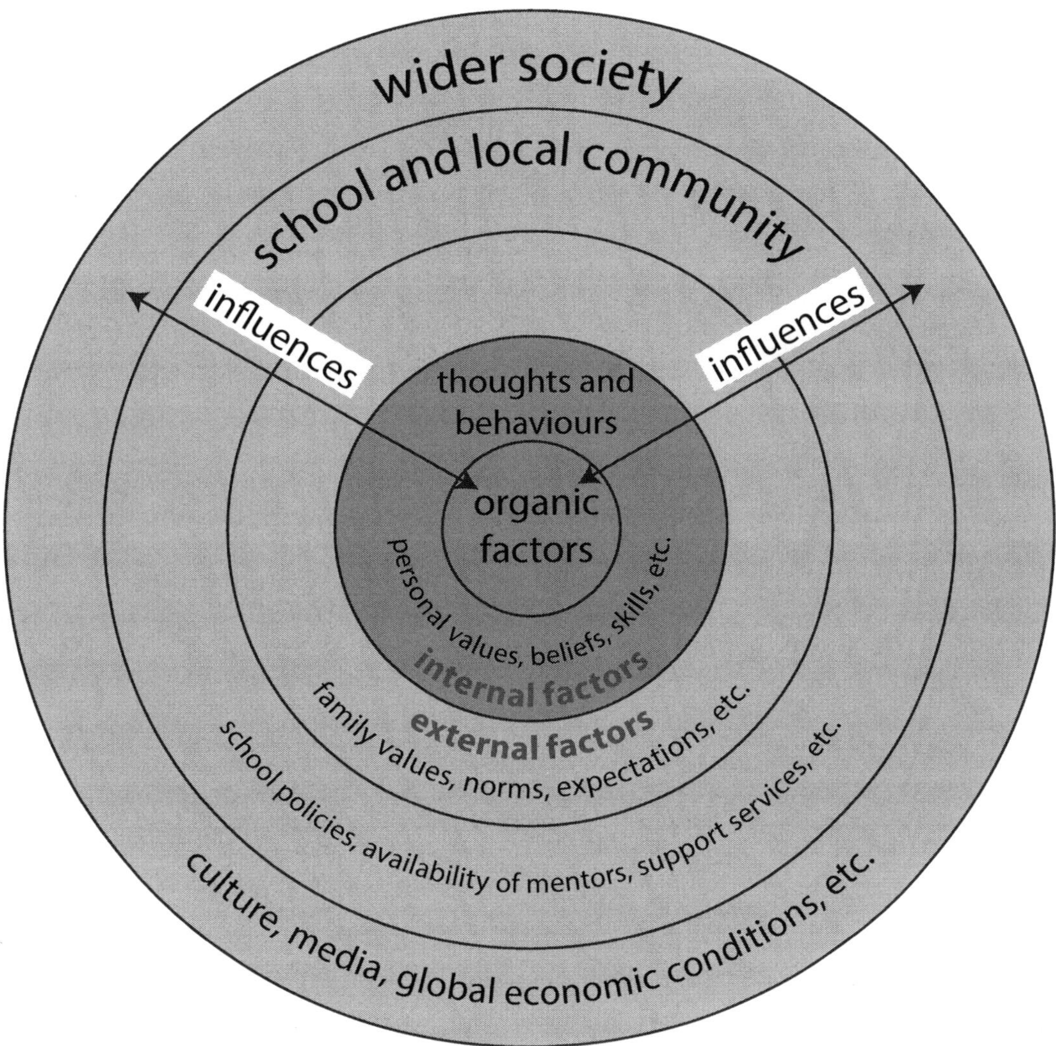


**Figure 1** The ecological perspective (Bronfenbrenner 1979)

As the diagram above illustrates, resilience is a function of a network of bi-directional influences that embrace the individual's inner world of thoughts and feelings, their family, school and immediate neighbourhood and, ultimately, the wider world, in which factors such as national mental health policies, global economic climate, terrorism and the media come into play.

This resource focuses primarily on developing the skill-set of adults dealing with children every day, since it is they who will support the young person in developing resilience, using both internal and external factors. The principles of Positive Psychology underpin this approach, as they highlight the importance of recognising and building upon the individual's own strengths and resources.

The book is divided into four parts, as follows:

## *Part 1 Building Resilience*

The text may be read sequentially, but it has been designed in a way that enables the reader – whether a parent or professional – to dip into topics whenever they seem most relevant.

## *Part 2 Activities*

These are designed to be used with individual children, or in small groups and whole classes. (All of the Activities are photocopiable for ease of use.)

## *Part 3 Handouts for Parents, Carers & Professionals*

This includes advice for parents, carers and professionals working with and supporting children in the early years.

## *Part 4 Recommended Reading & Resources for Parents, Carers & Professionals*

The publications in this list are relevant to the promotion of resilience and wellbeing in children and young people. Again, this enables the reader – whether a parent or professional – to dip into topics or follow up on a specific area whenever they seem most relevant.

# Part 1
# Building Resilience

# Building Resilience

## What is Resilience & Why is it so Important in the Early Years?

> [Resilience is]... a universal capacity that allows a person, group or community to prevent, minimise or overcome the damaging effects of adversity.
> — Grotberg, 'The International Resilience Project', 1997, p.6

Resilience, grit, self-control and character are terms that have been increasingly used in the context of education, health and wellbeing. 'Resilience' describes the inter-related components that support an individual's positive self-development: the capacity of an individual to restore good mental and emotional health, following the onset of challenging and adverse situations.

The word 'resilience' is derived from the Latin *resilio*, literally meaning 'to jump (or bounce) back'. Emotional resilience measures our ability to cope with or adapt to stressful situations or crises, be this a hurricane in Kathmandu or an A-level exam in Kimbolton. In essence, the two situations are not so different: rather, they are on a spectrum of adversity. Disasters are the exception. They take you closer to your levels of tolerance. How we cope with adversity and how we cope with catastrophe are best perceived as on a continuum.

It is vital is for all those supporting young people, whether in a social or learning context, to understand that emotional resilience can be taught. It is not simply those who have been exposed to natural disasters who develop it; nor is it only children who can surround themselves with its protective armour. Researchers have also found that adults are just as adept at learning the skills needed to be emotionally strong, proactive and decisive, no matter how late in life they start to realise the importance of these skills.

Ultimately, resilience is the ability to steer through serious life challenges and find ways to bounce back and to thrive. We are all born with the capacity for resilience, but resilience is not something we have or do not have. We work on it throughout our lives and we need to start as early as possible. Parents are probably the most important people when it comes to building a child's resilience, as children learn a great deal by watching their parents. When parents cope well with everyday stress, they are showing their children how to do the same. This can also be said of teachers and support staff in the early years. They are also pivotal in fostering resilience and doing so by both modelling and intervention work.

## *Why is it important to develop resilience?*

Resilience makes a big difference in people's lives. People who respond to hardships with resilience are:

- healthier and live longer
- happier in their relationships
- more successful in school and work
- less likely to get depressed

## *What are the key skills for resilience?*

- Self-awareness: understanding one's own emotions and needs, and being able to communicate these to others
- Self-control: managing anger and anxiety and the expression of emotions
- Social awareness: being aware of the needs and feelings of others, and building the capacity to respect those with different views or beliefs
- Social management: developing the skills and confidence to talk and mix with other children and adults, and to work and play well with others
- Responsibility: taking responsibility for a range of tasks, such as tidying up, doing homework and helping others
- Effort and persistence: understanding the importance of hard work and persistence
- Hope: believing in the possibility of a good future and in the value of education
- Self-esteem: feeling proud of the effort one makes at school, as well as efforts to get along with others and to be part of the family
- Problem-solving skills: building the capacity to think about how to deal with a range of challenges
- Positive coping strategies: developing the capacity to cheer oneself up, calm oneself down, to ask for help when needed, and to work out ways to solve a problem

## *What builds resilience?*

Many of the things that support healthy development in young children also help build their resilience. These things include:

- a secure bond or attachment with a caring adult, which forms in the early years
- relationships with positive role models
- opportunities to learn skills
- opportunities to participate in meaningful activities

Resilience is a skill that enables children and young people to survive and function, despite disadvantage and risk beyond that of the normal challenges of growing up. Masten (1999, 2007) describes resilience as 'ordinary magic'.

## Building Caring & Nurturing Relationships

### *Why are caring relationships important for resilience-building?*

> I have two older children who play football at a national level and so we're quite busy with that. I am also busy with college because I am taking a course in accountancy and I am also working at the same time. So, I am really trying to balance everything. Last week I was busy doing some homework before we went to football training; and I think my youngest child was feeling left out. She said, 'I want to play a game with you. We never play games together anymore.' So, I spent some time playing a game with her. It wasn't a long time, maybe 20 minutes or so. And I could see she felt better. It made her feel that I was listening to her, too. A lot of the time I think that children know when you are not really listening. So being able to really listen and spend time with them makes a big difference with your relationship.
>
> Parent

Building a close, loving relationship with your children is the most important thing you can do to support their resilience. Children do best when they feel loved, understood and accepted, and are protected from harm. Feeling wanted and loved helps us to get through the hard times in life and meet challenges and manage failures.

Children learn to feel safe and secure through a close attachment with at least one caring person. They also learn that their needs will be met. All of this gives them the confidence to explore their world.

Caring relationships provide accepting places where children can learn to regulate their:

- bodies
- feelings
- attention
- thoughts

- behaviour

Positive daily interactions with parents teach children how to have caring relationships with other important people in their lives. It also makes it easier for them to reach out to others when they need help.

## *Tips for building caring relationships*

- Give attention and affection – lots of smiles and hugs. This makes your children feel secure, loved and accepted.
- Play with your children. Playing together is a great way for you to connect, get to know them better and have fun. It is also a great way for children to develop physical, imagination and social skills.
- Comfort your children. When children are hurt or frightened, sad or angry, being comforted helps them feel as if they are not alone with their big or uncomfortable feelings. They will feel closer to you and learn healthy ways to comfort themselves and others as they get older.
- Listen with interest to your children's feelings, thoughts and ideas. This lets them know you think what they have to say is important.
- Show empathy. Empathy means seeing things from other people's point of view. This does not mean you have to agree with them. It just means that you are letting them know you understand how they feel. When children feel understood, it is easier for them to try to understand others. Empathy is the foundation for developing caring relationships with other people.
- Help your children identify and express their feelings (glad, sad, mad, scared, etc.). Point out that other people have these feelings, too.
- Reduce TV time. Children between 2 and 4 years should watch TV for less than 1 hour per day. Instead, find things to do that build your relationship, like reading together, making models, going swimming or going to the park.
- Read or tell your children stories about people who show compassion, kindness and understanding for others.

## *Be a positive role model*

Young children copy what others say and do. Parents and other adults can learn to be positive role models by handling difficult situations with resilience. When parents stay calm and flexible in dealing with life's challenges, they are teaching their children positive ways to handle stress. They

are also ensuring that children learn that life can present difficulties and challenges and that this is entirely normal. Managing stress effectively is a key aspect of resilience.

Tips for being a positive role model:

- Take care of your health. Show children that it is important to eat healthy foods, get enough sleep and exercise regularly. These reduce daily stress. They give us the mental and physical strength to deal with more serious challenges.
- Show understanding, compassion and kindness. Imagine what it is like to walk in other people's shoes.
- Take three deep breaths when you are stressed. Breathe in slowly to the count of three and then breathe out slowly to the count of three. Repeat three times to relax your body and get control of your emotions.
- Be in charge of your emotions. It is normal and appropriate to have all kinds of feelings. It is also healthy to express them in constructive ways.
- Be patient. Keep on trying even when things are frustrating, as this teaches children the value of grit and perseverance. Show patience with your children when they are trying and encourage them to keep trying.
- Let go of being perfect. Remember mistakes are just part of learning and that perfection does not exist. We can all only try to do and be our best. Encouraging the notion of 'personal bests' is very helpful.
- Stop and re-think. When things go wrong, try not to jump to conclusions. Ask yourself: 'How else can I think about this?' What parts can I control? What else can I do?' Take a moment before you respond.
- Take responsibility for your own feelings and actions in front of your children: 'Oops, I just made a mistake on this, but I can make up for it by doing …', or 'I'm sorry I shouted at you. Next time, I'm going to stop and calm down before I speak.'
- Use humour. It reduces stress and helps us look at challenging situations with a positive outlook.
- Stay positive. Enjoy simple pleasures. Look for the upside to challenges. This encourages us to keep trying. It also helps us learn from these experiences.
- Reach out for support. Everyone needs help sometimes and it is important to identify and make use of an appropriate support network.
- Reach out to help others who are going through difficult times.

## The Effects of Anxiety

Worry and anxiety are a part of life and the management of these feelings is a skill to be learnt and developed if we are able to fulfil our potential. All children and young people may, at times, need help and support in order to achieve this.

Sometimes it could be that their parents are indeed anxious themselves and have avoidant, overly protective styles of parenting that discourage age-appropriate 'fear-facing' behaviour and contribute to negative and unhelpful patterns or cycles of behaviour.

### *Cycles of anxiety in the lives of children*

#### 1 Social Life

Friendships are essential for children to learn and practise what they need to know to form lasting relationships. Friends also provide opportunities for fun and leisure, and friends can motivate each other to try new experiences.

When a child avoids school, a vicious cycle can become established because friendship dynamics can have changed, making joining in again more difficult, thereby creating further anxiety.

#### 2 Academic Performance

There is no reason to believe that children who suffer from anxiety are, on the whole, less bright than those children who do not. Despite this, children with anxiety can achieve less than their true potential, due to the following cyclical process:

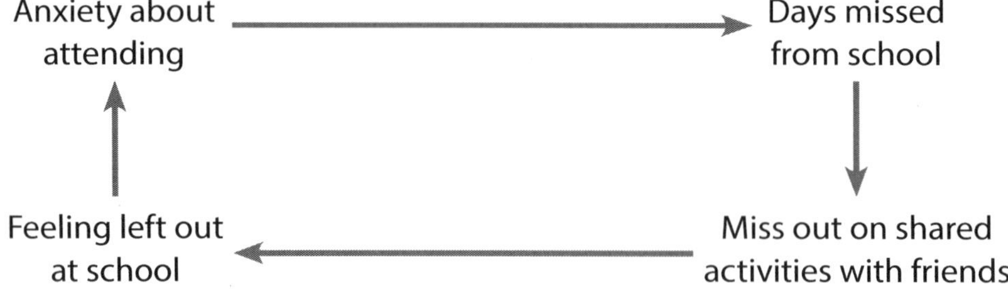


**Figure 2** Cycle of anxiety created by missing days at school

(Adapted from Cresswell & Willett, 2007, *Overcoming your Child's Fears and Worries*)

## 3 Mood

About half of children who experience significant anxiety problems also experience symptoms of low mood or depression, such as loss of interest in usual activities, tearfulness or irritability, feelings of worthlessness, and physical symptoms such as poor appetite and sleep problems.

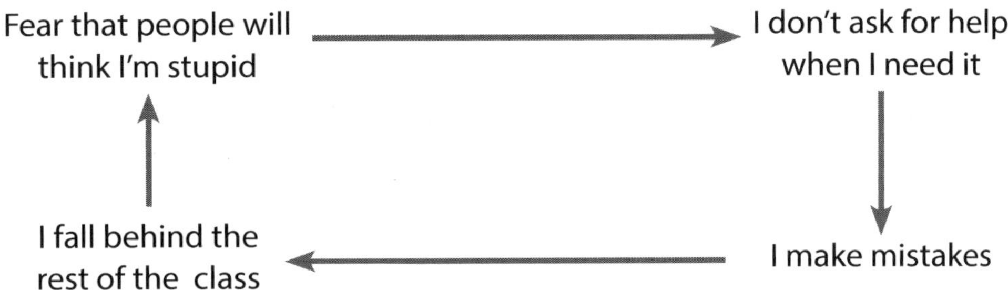


**Figure 3** The effects of anxiety on academic performance

## *Dealing with fear & anxiety*

Fear and anxiety cover a broad spectrum, including:

- Normal, everyday fears, such as the fear of being rejected, looking silly, getting into trouble, or being physically hurt.
- Exaggerated fears or phobias. Common childhood phobias include: the dark, animals, heights, storms, water and medical procedures.
- Shyness or social anxiety, which may or may not be clinically significant.
- Anxiety arising from trauma, including traumatic world events such as the events of 9/11, or the London and Paris terrorist attacks.

## Everyday fears

Part of resilience is the capacity to overcome fears that have arisen as the result of bad experiences. For example, a child who has had a bad experience performing in front of an audience may come to fear and avoid public performance in future. A child who can bounce back from such an experience by telling themselves that the bad experience is past and unlikely to be repeated – and understands the importance of 'feeling the fear and doing it anyway' – is demonstrating resilience (and courage). There are several strategies that can be used to help children overcome normal fears and develop courage.

1 Explain that courage means:
   - Doing something that one needs or wants to do, despite feeling anxious or uncomfortable about it.
   - Facing hardship or pain without giving up or being overwhelmed.
2 Explain that courage does not mean:
   - Doing something stupid or dangerous because someone dared you to.
   - Being 'tough' or showing off. Sometimes it might take courage to do something that others think is 'weak' or 'uncool'.
3 Praise children for being brave. Notice when children confront a fear successfully and praise them for it. Doing so repeatedly helps the child to establish an image of themselves as someone who is able to confront their fears and surmount them. It also helps them to establish a memory resource of the times when they were courageous, which they can then draw on when experiencing fear and anxiety. Adults can emphasise these positive memories by reminding them of past occasions when they were afraid, but were courageous and got past their fear without negative consequences.
4 Use self-talk. Show children how one can bolster one's courage by giving oneself a 'pep-talk' that challenges fearful thoughts. Developing helpful scripts is a useful strategy. Also, encourage children who have had a bad experience to confront their anxiety by going back into a similar situation soon after in order to learn that the bad experience is unlikely to be repeated.

## Phobias

Phobias in childhood are relatively common. Sometimes, but by no means always, such phobias begin with a frightening experience. Sometimes phobias seem to develop spontaneously for no apparent reason. Unlike adults, who recognise that their phobic reaction is unreasonable or out of proportion to the threat, children and young people often do not. They also may not express their fear directly, but show it in their behaviour by avoiding feared situations, clinging to adults, crying, and so on.

Phobias, in both adults and children, are typically treated by a process of gradual desensitisation, in which the phobic person is supported to confront their fear in manageable doses. For example, to treat a fear of spiders, a person might at first simply be exposed to descriptions of spiders. Then, when they can cope with this level of exposure, they might be shown photographs of spiders, and so on, until they are actually capable of touching a spider without a phobic response.

This process of desensitisation should generally be undertaken by a trained professional, but parents and carers can help a child to draw up a hierarchy in the form of a ladder, with the least anxiety-provoking part of the situation or fear at the bottom and the feared object at the top. This enables the child to take smaller steps to confronting and eventually managing the phobia. Visualising the problem in smaller, successive steps is an effective strategy and enables the child or young person to remain positive by breaking down what may seem an extremely challenging task into smaller and more manageable steps.

## Shyness & social anxiety

People vary in their natural degree of sociability or extraversion. Some children and young people are naturally shy. While it is important to recognise and accept this variation, shy children do face social disadvantages as a result of their introversion. Shy people tend to have more negative self-perceptions than extraverts. They also tend to have poorer health (as a result of more limited social support networks), be lonelier, and earn less money than their more socially at-ease peers. It therefore makes sense to help shy children to become more comfortable in social situations. The following are some strategies that can help:

1. Do not be over-protective
   It is tempting to protect shy children from situations that arouse anxiety for them. However, this is a mistake, as it tends to reinforce the shyness and limit further social development. Parents should continue to hold reasonable expectations and encourage their child to confront situations that arouse anxiety for them.

2. Set goals
   Setting goals and offering rewards can help a child to gradually overcome shyness. When going into a new situation, parents can set small, achievable goals for their child and then offer a reward for achieving these.

3. Avoid labelling
   Labelling a child as 'shy' can result in the child coming to define him or herself this way, and hence reinforce the shyness and the sense of being somehow 'wrong'. It is more helpful to use words like 'reserved', if labels need to be used at all.

**4** Avoid judging
Shy children are typically frightened of being judged, so making negative judgments about a child's shy behaviour can be particularly counter-productive. Rather than attacking the child for their shy behaviour, reward them for coming out of their shell and making the effort to socialise or engage with others.

**5** Do not push too hard
Whilst it is important to gently challenge a shy child to go out of their comfort zone in order to develop confidence and social skills, pushing a child too hard can result in them being flooded with anxiety and becoming even more afraid of social situations. It can also result in a power struggle developing between the child and their parents. Extraverted parents, in particular, can sometimes have difficulty in understanding their child's temperament and fall into the trap of becoming too pushy. Rather than pushing a child to come out of themselves, it is usually a more productive approach to try to foster an atmosphere of acceptance and warmth, within which the child feels safe enough to start expressing themselves spontaneously.

**6** Teach social skills
Shy children are particularly in need of explicit teaching of social skills. This can be done via modelling and also by direct intervention work from professionals in both the school and clinical contexts. Many school-based staff will undertake small-group social skills work and such interventions have an increasing evidence base in terms of effectively building children's skills and ensuring their social inclusion.

## Managing fear in an age of terror

The climate of fear created by recent and on-going acts of terrorism around the world creates new mental health challenges, especially when children are exposed to images that are replayed endlessly on television or via social media. The following are some tips for helping children to manage their anxiety in the face of frightening or traumatic world events:

- Limit exposure to horrifying images. It is very difficult to shield children completely from the graphic media images of trauma and suffering following a terrorist attack or natural disaster, especially as children grow older. Children, like adults, may feel a curious compulsion to view such images, despite being disturbed or upset by them. Nevertheless, exposure to such footage can create serious anxiety reactions in children, especially if such exposure is repeated and/or prolonged.

- Take time to explain events rationally to children. In doing so, it is important to take into consideration the age and level of understanding of the child and limit explanations to what can be assimilated at the child's developmental stage. Allow children time to ask questions and express their emotional reactions. Also, be sure to normalise the reaction, for example:

'Yes. It is normal to feel frightened and sad about this. Everyone will feel like this, as it is such a horrible event.'

- Make sure children know some ways of reducing anxiety, such as using relaxation techniques and Mindfulness approaches and strategies.
- Help children to feel safe by continuing normal routines, providing reassurance and explaining the very low likelihood of such traumatic events. Because of the dramatic nature of tragedies such as 9/11 or the Paris and London attacks, it is easy to forget the millions of safe flights, safe buildings and unharmed people who did not make the news.
- Monitor anxiety levels in children, including signs such as nightmares, sleeplessness, and physical symptoms such as stomach upsets, tearfulness and phobias. Depression and anger can also manifest as reactions to trauma. If signs of anxiety are severe or do not disappear fairly quickly after the event, then it is wise to seek professional support. Be aware that in many instances, signs of traumatic reaction may not appear until several months after the initial event.

## Understanding the Impact & Importance of Attachment Theory in Building Resilience

'Attachment' is the deep connection established between a child and caregiver: it profoundly affects a child's development and ability to express emotions and develop relationships and resilience. Parents, carers and teachers who support and nurture those with an attachment disorder are likely to experience significant levels of stress and sometimes feel exhausted from trying to connect with a child with such difficulties. A child with insecure attachment or an attachment disorder lacks the skills for building meaningful relationships, but we now know that with a great deal of effort, nurture, patience and love, it is possible repair attachment challenges.

### *Causes of attachment disorders*

Reactive attachment disorder and other attachment problems occur when children have been unable to consistently connect with a parent or primary caregiver. This can happen for many reasons:

1. A baby cries and no one responds or offers comfort.
2. A baby is hungry or wet, and they are not attended to for hours.
3. No one looks at, talks to, or smiles at the baby, so the baby feels alone.
4. A young child gets attention only when it acts out or displays other extreme behaviours.
5. A young child or baby is mistreated or abused.
6. Sometimes the child's needs are met and sometimes they are not. The child never knows what to expect.
7. The infant or young child is hospitalised, or separated from their parents.
8. A baby or young child is moved from one caregiver to another (perhaps as the result of adoption, foster care, or the loss of a parent).
9. The parent is emotionally unavailable because of depression, an illness, or a substance abuse problem.

As the examples show, sometimes the circumstances that cause the attachment problems are unavoidable, but the child is too young to understand what has happened and why. To a young child, it just feels like no one cares and they lose trust in others – the world becomes an unsafe place.

## *Signs & symptoms of insecure attachment*

Attachment problems fall on a spectrum, from mild problems that are easily addressed to the most serious form, known as reactive attachment disorder (RAD).

Although it is never too late to treat and repair attachment difficulties such as reactive attachment disorder, the earlier we can identify the symptoms of insecure attachment and take steps to remedy the condition, the better. With early detection, we can avoid a more serious problem in the longer term. Caught in infancy, attachment problems are often easy to correct – particularly when the right help and support is made available, both in the home and the learning contexts.

An infant suffering from attachment disorder may:

1. avoid eye contact
2. not smile

3 not reach out to be picked up

4 reject efforts to calm, soothe and connect

5 not appear to notice or care when left alone

6 cry inconsolably

7 not coo or make any sound

8 not follow an adult with their eyes

9 Show no interest in interactive games or playing with toys

10 spend a lot of time rocking or comforting themselves

It is important to note that the early symptoms of insecure attachment are similar to the early symptoms of other issues such as ADHD and autism. When parents and carers spot any of these warning signs, it is therefore vital that they make an appointment with the paediatrician for a professional diagnosis of the problem and to access appropriate support and intervention.

## *The importance of an approach informed by attachment theory*

Early developmental experiences with caregivers – the infant's first exposure to humans – create a set of associations and 'templates' for the child's brain: a concept of what humans 'are'. Are humans safe, predictable? Are they a source of sustenance, comfort and pleasure? Or are they unpredictable and a source of fear, chaos, pain and loss?' (Perry & Hambrick, 2008)

An understanding of attachment theory is clearly crucial in supporting the needs of our children and young people. John Bowlby (1969) initially outlined his theory of attachment over 50 years ago, highlighting how important a secure attachment is in terms of the development of the child. Why is this process of attachment so important? Although attachment is significant throughout the human life span, the special bond that develops between an infant and primary caregiver in the first 12 months of life is usually seen as the template for future relationship experiences. Babies will experience this bond in terms of safety, comfort and pleasure needs being met. They will also show very real distress when they feel that this relationship has been lost, even for a very short period of time. When young children are upset, nervous or anxious, they will attempt to remain in close proximity to their significant caregiver and will have a clear and secure strategy for gaining this kind of closeness. We know that this attachment is mainly influenced by the quality and characteristics of their primary care giver(s). Sensitive and reliable responses to a child's distress will ensure a more secure attachment

## *Attachment theory & neuroscience*

> The experience of a prolonged insecure attachment, whatever the cause, has long been suspected of producing 'invisible damage'. New methods of measurement in neuropsychology and neurobiology have been able to quantify this damage in terms of brain growth and activity. In short, we now know that parental rejection, abuse and neglect not only cause grievous developmental harm, but also grievous bodily harm.
>
> Cameron & Maginn, 2008

What we now know from neuroscience is that traumatic early experiences can alter the architecture of the brain itself. Perry and Hambrick (2008) argue that the brain develops in a neurosequential way, starting at the brain stem, which governs basic physiological survival behaviours, right up to the frontal cortex, which is the seat of conscious thought. The brain will therefore develop differently, according to the kind of stimulation it receives. This stimulation comes via the physical, sensory, social and emotional environment in which a child is nurtured. The patterned rhythmic activities associated with sensitive, attuned parenting produce a well-organised functional brain, but for an infant who receives chaotic or no real stimulation, the brain will present with a lack of neurological connectedness and chaotic or dysfunctional organisation.

On a more optimistic note, the researchers have also been able to detect the ways in which some of this resulting damage can subsequently be repaired as a direct result of more positive experiences and attuned and nurturing care-giving. This is the scientific evidence to support the approach of attachment-informed care-giving. In this approach there is therefore a focus on recognising the damage, particularly in terms of learning and emotional development, and in making the right kind of adjustments and differentiating approaches to learning and behaviour management in both the home and school context. For example, carers and parents will need to be able to respond to children at their emotional age, rather than their chronological one.

Interventions and support systems for children should aim to address developmental brain impairment by providing care that can build fundamental brain capacities. For many children this will mean less use of verbal techniques and a greater concentration on physical, sensory and emotional ways of working and supporting them. There will also need to be a focus on using the relationship between child and carer to address the developmental deficits and likely neurological impairments experienced by the child. This may involve focusing on touch, sensory stimulation, music and play, alongside providing a safe, predictable routine and environment for the child. This will, in turn, ensure that the carer or parent can support the child or young person to recognise and manage feelings, and to also develop the capacity to understand their own mental state and that of others (to 'mentalise'). This will then enable them to begin to make positive relationships with others and to also begin to focus and learn within both the home and the school context.

## *Advice for those supporting a child with attachment disorder*

- Have realistic expectations. Helping the child with an attachment disorder may be a long road. Focus on taking small steps forward and celebrate every sign of success.
- Patience is essential. The process may not be as rapid as we might like, and we can expect bumps along the way. However, by remaining patient and focusing on small improvements, we can create an atmosphere of safety for the child.
- Foster a sense of humour and joy. Joy and humour go a long way toward repairing attachment problems and energising you even in the midst of a great deal of hard work. Try to find at least a couple of people or activities that help you laugh and feel good on a daily basis and timetable these into your day.
- Take care of yourself and learn how to manage stress more effectively. Reduce other demands on your time and make time for yourself. Rest, good nutrition and breaks from the caring role help you relax and recharge your batteries so you can give your genuine attention to the child without any sense of resentment.
- Find support and ask for help. Rely on friends, family, community resources and respite care (if available). Try to ask for help before you really need it to avoid getting stressed to breaking point. You may also want to consider joining a support group for carers/parents/professionals who support attachment-disordered children and young people.
- Stay positive and hopeful. Be sensitive to the fact that children pick up on feelings. If they sense you are discouraged, it will be discouraging to them. When you are feeling down, turn to others for reassurance and build up a support network that enables you to avoid a sense of burnout and thus reduces the risk of 'blocked' care.

## *Helping children with attachment disorder feel safe & secure*

Safety is the core issue for children with attachment disorder and other attachment problems. They are distant and distrustful because they feel unsafe in the world. They keep their guard up to protect themselves, but this also prevents them from accepting love and support. So, before anything else, it is essential to build up the child's sense of security. You can accomplish this by establishing clear expectations and rules of behaviour, and by responding consistently so that the child knows what to expect when he or she acts a certain way and – even more importantly – knows that no matter what happens, you can be relied upon and will not reject them.

- Set limits and boundaries. Consistent, loving boundaries make the world seem more predictable and less scary to children with attachment problems such as reactive attachment disorder. It is important that they understand what behaviour is expected of them, what is and is not acceptable, and what the consequences will be if they disregard the rules. This also teaches them that they have more control over what happens to them than they think.

- Take control, yet remain calm when the child is upset or misbehaving. Remember that all behaviour is a form of communication and that negative behaviour means that the child does not know how to handle what they are feeling and needs your help. By staying calm, you show the child that the feeling is manageable. If they are being purposefully defiant, follow through with the pre-established consequences in a cool, matter-of-fact manner. However, never discipline a child with an attachment disorder when you are in an emotionally-charged state: this makes the child feel more unsafe and may even reinforce the unwanted behaviour, because it is clear that their behaviour has pushed your buttons and increased your stress levels.
- Be immediately available to reconnect following a conflict. Conflict can be especially disturbing for children with insecure attachment or attachment disorders. After a conflict or tantrum when you have had to discipline the child, be ready to reconnect as soon as they are ready. This reinforces your consistency and love, and will help the child develop a trust that you will be there for them at all times.
- Own up to mistakes and initiate repair. When you let frustration or anger get the best of you or you do something you realise is insensitive, quickly address the mistake. Your willingness to take responsibility and make amends can strengthen the attachment bond. Children with reactive attachment disorder or other attachment problems need to learn that although you may not be perfect, they will be loved, no matter what.
- Try to maintain predictable routines and schedules. A child with an attachment disorder will not instinctively rely on loved ones, and may feel threatened by transition and inconsistency, for example, when travelling or during school holidays. A familiar routine or schedule can provide comfort during times of change.

## *Reinforcing the child's positive experience of love & physical nurture*

A child who has not bonded early in life will have a hard time accepting love, especially any physical expressions of love. But you can help them learn to accept your love with time, consistency and repetition. Trust and security come from seeing loving actions, hearing reassuring words and feeling comforted over and over again.

- Find things that feel good to the child. If possible, show the child love through rocking, cuddling, and holding – attachment experiences they missed out on earlier. But always be respectful of what feels comfortable and good to the child. In cases of previous abuse and trauma, you may have to undertake this task in a very gradual and sensitive way, because the child may be very resistant to physical touch.

- Respond to the child's emotional age. Children with attachment disorders often act like younger children, both socially and emotionally. You may need to treat them as though they were much younger, using more non-verbal methods of soothing and comforting.
- Help the child identify emotions and express their needs. Children with attachment disorders may not know what they are feeling or how to ask for what they need. Reinforce the idea that all feelings are okay and show them healthy ways to express their emotions. Learn how to be an emotion coach and teach the child how to self-soothe, self-regulate and engage in effective problem-solving when they experience an overwhelmingly uncomfortable feeling.
- Listen, talk, and play with the child. Schedule times when you are able to give them your full, focused attention in ways that feel comfortable to them. It may seem hard to drop everything, eliminate distractions, and just be in the moment, but quality time together provides a great opportunity for the child to open up to you and feel your focused attention and care.
- A healthy diet is an essential. Make sure your child eats a diet full of whole grains, fruits, vegetables and lean protein. Be sure to skip the sugar and add plenty of good fats – like fish, flax seed, avocados and olive oil—for optimal brain health.
- A consistent sleeping pattern is always needed. If the child is tired during the day, it will be that much harder for them to focus on learning new things. Make their sleep schedule (bedtime and waking-up time) consistent.
- A regular amount of physical exercise. Exercise or any type of physical activity can be a great antidote to stress, frustration and pent-up emotion, triggering endorphins to make the child feel good. Physical activity is especially important for the angry child. If your child is not naturally active, try different classes or sports to find something that is appealing.

## The Self-Esteem Myth

Self-esteem has always been a vital area for development in young people, and one that has been frequently misunderstood and demonised by some members of the psychological community. Why is it so important? 'It is because children learn well with a combination of appropriately high expectations and appropriately high self-esteem' (Roberts, 2002, p.5).

In order to develop this self-esteem and the resilience associated with it, children as learners need to be able to take risks; this process must involve failure and the need for young people to be able to cope with the associated frustration. We therefore need to focus on preventing students from engaging in a negative learning cycle, for example: 'I worry about failing'; 'I will not succeed'; or 'I won't bother trying'.

It is important, at the same time, to note that the relationship between academic achievements and self-esteem can be rather confusing. Does good self-esteem raise achievement, or does achievement raise self-esteem? This is rather a chicken and egg situation. What is evident, however, is the fact that children who believe in their abilities tend to achieve more, in other words, their high self-esteem becomes a self-fulfilling prophecy.

## *Key terms*

There continues to be some confusion about the terms 'self-concept', 'ideal self', 'self-esteem' and 'global self-esteem'.

- 'Self-concept' is really the perception that a person has of themselves, or how they define themselves. For example: I'm a boy; I'm Arthur's best mate; I play football; I like Big Macs.' My own self-concept would be that I am a woman, I am loyal, I like writing and going to the gym, and I love good wine and malt whiskey. It is these individual components that make up the person.
- The 'ideal self' is what or who I would really like to be, and this is usually an idea that is formulated in comparison to others.
- 'Self-esteem', in effect, is the evaluation of those parts that make up the self-concept. For example: how much do I value being Arthur's mate? How important is it to have friends?
- 'Global self-esteem' is the overall feeling that we have towards ourselves. There will be specific areas where we feel good about ourselves and others when we're not so positive – this is perfectly normal.

## *Low self-esteem*

Low self-esteem has many causes and can be linked to distorted self-evaluation. Teasing or bullying by peers can trigger attachment issues, which often lead to an inferiority complex. Low self-esteem is also frequently caused by a poor ability to communicate, which limits the success of a student's social interactions. What is important to remember, however, is that experiencing low self-esteem at some point in our lives is completely normal.

## *'Depersonalised' self-esteem*

Some psychologists have put forward the view that self-esteem is becoming depersonalised; in other words, there is an increasingly prevalent belief that your low self-esteem is nothing to do with you and you are simply a victim. This distortion is based on the urge to shift blame for low self-esteem away from ourselves: it is not our fault – we are helpless and high self-esteem is our right.

When working with children and young people, however, it is important is to ensure that they are aware of the fact that they need to take responsibility for their feelings, beginning with their actions. A person's self-esteem will rise when their actions display some merit, since self-esteem is the outcome of what we do and is influenced by the choices we make for ourselves. This is quite a powerful concept, but one that is important for young people to grasp.

## *'Feel good' self-esteem*

A further argument put forward by some psychologists is that making oneself or others feel special by using methods such as looking in the mirror and saying, 'I am somebody', does not actually do any good – in fact it may actually do harm. This type of self-esteem building produces counterfeit positive self-assessment, which can consequently set people up for disappointment in the real world, since we may develop an unrealistic picture of our specialness.

## *The resilience route to authentic self-esteem*

Nan Henderson developed a resiliency route to authentic self-esteem that she describes as 'not being the stuff of meaningless affirmations' (1999, p.26). Having worked with young children and young people for many years in a range of educational and learning contexts, we have found it to be a hugely convincing and productive argument.

It is based upon: recognising actual accomplishments; identifying and understanding how we can make use of our strengths; living a life where we express our talents and gifts. These processes involve a shift in thinking for both adults and young people working to improve self-esteem. It is entirely solution-focused. There is an appreciation of how and why we have done as well as we have done, and there is also a recognition of the need to draw on innate capacity for overcoming adversity and bouncing back. Key questions here, for both adults and young people, are as follows:

- How have I done as well as I've done?
- What are the two or three biggest challenges, including crisis or traumas, I've overcome in my life?
- What did I use to overcome them?
- What do I use every day to effectively cope with the typical stresses in my life?

## Personal 'resilience builders'

It is essential that young people learn how to develop their own personal resilience builders in order to overcome adversity. Individual qualities that facilitate resilience are as follows:

- Ability to form relationships
- Humour
- Inner direction
- Perceptiveness
- Independence
- Positive view of personal future
- Flexibility
- Love of learning
- Self-motivation
- Competence
- Self-awareness
- Spirituality
- Perseverance
- Creativity

It is important for individuals to recognise the personal resilience builders that they use most frequently. Do they rely upon relationships and the ability to be a friend and form a positive relationship? Do they use humour to deflect difficult situations and feelings? Are they able to adjust to change, and bend as necessary in order to positively cope with a range of situations? Are they able to use creative outlets in order to express themselves? Building this kind of self-awareness is particularly important when young people are developing in all these areas. They require prompting to consider their skills and to reflect upon how they can be further developed.

## The importance of old messages!

Although these tactics all represent positives moves away from simple 'feel good' self-esteem towards authentic self-esteem, which involves choices and responsibilities, there remains a clear need to support the development of this kind of authentic self-esteem across a school community. Strategies that provide support include:

- Valuing attempts that children make, but not in an over-the-top manner, particularly in the case of those who have social, emotional, behavioural difficulties. This needs to be done discreetly and can often involve a mere look or positive comment.
- Providing students with 'helper' roles, from which their commitment and contribution will be valued.
- Allowing students to make choices and be responsible in the learning context.
- Developing personal records of success.
- Avoiding comparisons that can be damaging to individuals.
- Teaching the skills for emotional literacy and resilience in order to foster self-awareness and self-concept.
- Teaching and modelling the skills and strategies of cognitive behavioural therapy, solution-focused brief therapy and motivational interviewing in order to promote resilience and self-esteem.
- Promoting personal resilience builders, as described above.
- Building positive relationships with peers and adults in both the school and social communities.

## *Fourteen ways to enhance self-esteem*

These are common sense strategies, clearly not rocket science – but it can be all too easy to forget the importance of such simple ideas:

1. Spend time with people who like you and care about you.
2. Ignore and stay away from people who put you down or treat you badly.
3. Do things that you enjoy or that make you feel good.
4. Do things you are good at.
5. Reward yourself for your successes.
6. Develop your talents and skills.
7. Be your own best friend and treat yourself well, doing things that are good for you.
8. Make choices for yourself and do not let others make those choices for you.
9. Take responsibility for yourself, your choices and your actions.
10. Always do what you believe is right.

**11** Be true to yourself and your values.

**12** Respect other people and treat them right.

**13** Set goals and work to achieve them

**14** Do not beat yourself up when you get it wrong.

## Thinking Skills

In building our resilience and that of our children, the development of 'thinking skills' is vital. This is because the way we react to things has a lot to do with the way we think about the situation. That is why thinking skills play a big part in our ability to regulate our emotions and behaviour. Here's an example:

> Crystal, Katrina's 2-year-old daughter, has a tantrum in the shopping centre. Katrina thinks to herself, 'This is embarrassing. Everyone thinks I am a terrible mother. And it is all her father's fault for always giving in to her. He spoils her rotten.'
>
> These thoughts make Katrina feel embarrassed about the situation and angry at her partner and child. She grits her teeth, grabs Crystal's hand and pulls her out of the shopping centre. Crystal wails even louder and everyone stares as they go by. Both Katrina and her daughter are terribly upset. Katrina's anger grows and she can't wait to have a real 'go' at her partner for spoiling Crystal.

We all jump to conclusions about *why* difficult situations happen in our lives. When we're looking at what *caused* the situation, we often blame someone. We blame ourselves or others for our problems.

Instead of jumping to conclusions, it is very useful to follow three easy steps in order to identify and understand what is really happening and why we are responding in the way that we do. These steps help us respond to stressful situations effectively, using our ability to think rationally as opposed to simply reacting or even over-reacting and catastrophising. In the example of Katrina, this process might look as follows:

| | |
|---|---|
| Step 1 | Stop and catch your thoughts:<br>*'This is embarrassing. Everyone thinks I am a terrible mother. And it's all her father's fault for always giving in to her. He spoils her terribly.'* |
| Step 2 | Take three deep breaths:<br>*'Wait a minute, this isn't helpful. I need to take some deep breaths so I can be calm enough to calm her down.'* |
| Step 3 | 'Rethink' the situation by asking yourself: how else can I think about this?<br>*'It's really hot and crowded in here. And it's almost nap time. Crystal is probably just trying to tell me this is too much for her. After all, she's only two.'* |

So, Katrina picks up Crystal, and in a soothing voice says, 'It's okay. I know you are hot and tired. Let's go home and have a cuddle and a nap.' Although Crystal does not stop crying immediately, she has calmed down by the time they leave the shopping centre. Mother and daughter feel connected and Katrina decides she won't take Crystal to the shops again so close to nap time.

Katrina used what we would describe as 'flexible' thinking in order to respond to the situation instead of reacting to her first thoughts. She realised blaming her daughter or partner was not going to help the situation and was ultimately counterproductive. Instead, she was able to:

- calm herself down and calm Crystal, too
- realise Crystal was tired and hot, but too young to express this with words
- plan for future trips to the shopping centre
- avoid an unnecessary argument with her partner.

Helping children develop thinking skills is clearly best done in a caring relationship in which the parent/carer can model emotionally literate and self-regulated behaviours. This modelling and way of responding to a child's behaviours and moods is an important part of supporting the development of the child's own self-regulation.

Some tips for helping children of 3 years plus develop thinking skills:

- Help children talk about their thoughts. Often when we ask children to tell us what they are thinking, they shrug their shoulders and say, 'I don't know.' However, questions like, 'What are you saying to yourself inside your head?', or 'What is your head telling you?', often help children to express thoughts that cause their feelings and, subsequently, their behaviours.
- For example, a child who refuses to get dressed in the morning may be able to tell us what is actually causing this behaviour. 'I hate going to Nursery! Everyone takes my toys. No one wants to play with me. I hate Nursery!'
- Gently challenge your children's negative thinking.
- 'Always thinking' such as, 'Jack always wants to play with someone else', can be turned around by pointing out the times the child has played with Jack.
- 'Everything thinking' such as, 'Now everything is ruined', can be changed by helping your child see that if one thing goes wrong, it does not mean that everything is ruined. Or, if one person does not want to play, it does not mean that no one wants to play.

- Play thinking games together. Children can benefit from playing games that help them think, such as: 'What would happen if ...?' Games like these help children think about their actions and how to handle situations in a positive way.
- Encourage children to imagine another way to do something – perhaps a different way to join others at the playground, play with toys or tidy up. This helps them learn there is usually more than one way to do things.
- Read or tell children stories about how others overcome obstacles, get along with others or turn a difficult situation around. You can use puppets or stuffed animals to help bring the story alive. This helps to normalise the idea that we all face challenges and there is usually a way to overcome them if we stop, think and reflect in a more rational and solution-focused way.

## Emotional Literacy

'Emotional literacy' is the term used to describe the ability to understand and express feelings. Emotional literacy as a term was first used by Steiner and Perry (1997). It refers to:

> ... the ability to understand your emotions, the ability to listen to others and empathise with their emotions, and the ability to express emotions productively. To be emotionally literate is to be able to handle emotions in a way that improves your personal power and improves the quality of life around you. Emotional literacy improves relationships, creates loving possibilities between people, makes co-operative work possible, and facilitates the feeling of community.
>
> Steiner & Perry, 1997, p. 11

Emotional literacy involves having self-awareness and recognition of one's own feelings and knowing how to manage them, such as the ability to stay calm when angered or to reassure oneself when in doubt. It includes empathy (having sensitivity to the feelings of other people) and it has been said that emotionally literate people are able to employ self-discipline in order to harness their emotions and identify and reach their personal goals.

Emotional literacy also includes being able to recognise and adapt to the feelings of other people, whilst at the same time learning how to manage and express one's own emotions effectively. This is helpful to developing good communication skills and the enhancement of our relationships with other people.

It is especially important that young children develop emotional literacy because they need to have a recognition of their emotions in order to know how to behave, mature and ultimately be happy. Using emotion coaching approaches, as described below, is crucial to ensuring the development of these skills in children and young people.

Emotional literacy could ultimately be defined as the ability to recognise, understand, handle and appropriately express your emotions and this includes the following:

- being aware of what you are feeling
- understanding why you might be feeling that way
- knowing the most effective way for expressing your feelings and being able to actually carry out this response
- understanding and taking into account the feelings of others and adjusting your responses accordingly.

These four areas of emotional literacy are the key ones on which we need to focus as professionals and parents/carers working with children and young people. We need to ensure that we ourselves have these skills in order to effectively support the development of them in those that we care for.

## Recognising, Naming & Managing Emotions

Even adults sometimes need help to identify what they are feeling. It should not be surprising, then, that children need to be taught an 'affective vocabulary' in order to begin to learn the complex skills of regulating and communicating about emotion.

### *The four basic emotions*

The simplest emotional vocabulary of all consists of four words for the four fundamental human emotions: SAD (sad, blue, gloomy), MAD (angry, irritable, furious), BAD (guilty, anxious, fearful) and GLAD (happy, joyous, peaceful, content). Although it is not clear that these four words cover all human emotions (surprise and disgust, for example, seem to be basic emotions that are not covered), they are nonetheless a very simple and easily understood mnemonic for younger children to use to label their emotions.

An important understanding for children to learn is that emotions can be mixed. For example, it is quite possible to feel sad and glad at the same time – one example is the pleasantly melancholy feeling that a sad and beautiful piece of music can evoke. One can also feel mad and glad (angry and happy) at the same time, for example in the thrill of intense competition during sport – witness the expressions of many sports stars upon winning a major event.

Identifying emotions as sad, mad, glad and bad can also become the basis for teaching children basic emotional regulation skills.

## Using emojis to teach emotion recognition

The understanding of human facial expressions has been found to be universal across cultures. An angry, happy, sad, frightened, surprised, or disgusted expression will have the same basic characteristics and will be recognised accurately regardless of the culture in which it occurs. An easy way to teach an emotional vocabulary to children is through emojis – the little expressive faces that often adorn internet communications. Even without an emotional vocabulary, young children can point to a face that expresses what they are feeling. They can then learn to associate this with the appropriate word.

### *Teaching emotional self-acceptance*

Because of the social undesirability of inappropriate expressions of anger and other negative emotions, it is easy for children to form the impression that certain emotions are intrinsically 'bad'. Part of teaching children an affective vocabulary should include teaching them that all emotions are acceptable. However, acting out those emotions in certain ways may not be. Sometimes this can be a hard distinction for younger children to grasp, especially in relation to anger, which is the least socially acceptable emotion to express and the one most likely to meet with consistent negative reactions from adults.

It is particularly difficult for children to learn to accept the full range of their emotional responses if the adults around them are unable to accept those emotions, or their own emotional states. Emotional self-acceptance begins with adults who genuinely accept the right of each child to his or her own sadness, fear, anger and joy, and patiently teach children how to regulate these emotions, not suppress them.

### *Managing anger*

Most children learn to control their anger naturally as they get older. Physical expressions of aggression decline for most children between the ages of three and five. However, for some children, problems with regulating anger continue into the school years and may cause social problems. There are several techniques that children can be taught to manage anger.

## Recognising when I'm angry

The first step in managing anger is recognising the signs of anger and knowing when there is a danger of it 'boiling over'. One way to help children learn to recognise the warning signs of an angry outburst is to draw an anger thermometer, marked with degrees of anger from 1–10, with labels going from 'calm' (1), to 'annoyed' (5), to 'angry' (10). The child can then be asked what situations they can think of in which they felt that angry, and what they noticed in their body at the time. This might include:

- Feeling hot in the face or tummy
- Clenching the jaw
- Shaking
- 'Seeing red'

You can then ask them at what point on the anger thermometer there is a danger of them losing their temper and lashing out. Note that some children are volatile and reach the explosion point very quickly. These children may find it hard to monitor their anger. The most effective approach for these children may simply be repeated reinforcement of the unacceptability of violent behaviour, with appropriate and consistent consequences.

## Techniques to reduce anger

Once children can recognise the warning signs that they are getting angry, they can learn various ways of reducing the anger and preventing an outburst.

1. **Time out** Time out means simply taking a break from the situation: walking away and taking a break until one has cooled down. Alternatively one can count slowly from 1 to 10 to allow a surge of anger to pass.
2. **Deep breathing** Breathing slowly and deeply has a calming effect on the emotions. To implement this technique effectively, children need to practise it and get used to it when they are feeling calm. Note that fast, deep breathing actually creates anxiety, so make sure that the breath is comfortable and relaxed.
3. **Seeking adult support** Young children who have difficulty resolving conflicts with peers alone should be encouraged to seek adult support to assist them to resolve any conflict.
4. **Relaxation** Relaxation techniques can help children to discharge a build-up of anger and tension. See 'Relax & Unwind', below, for more information.
5. **Switching channels** One technique that has been employed with children is to get children to make television sets out of cardboard and paper, with different sheets of coloured paper to represent different feelings or 'channels'. Children are then taught that if they are on the 'angry' channel they can switch over to the 'calm' channel.

6 **The 'Turtle Technique'** The turtle technique is a technique from Cognitive Behavioural Therapy that combines a number of anger and impulse control strategies into a simple technique that can easily be used with children as young as 3 or 4 (Robin, Schneider & Dolnick, 1976). There are four steps to the technique:

- **a** Recognising that one is angry (help children to do this by getting them to identify the physical signs of anger).
- **b** Thinking 'stop'.
- **c** Going into one's 'shell' and taking three deep breaths and thinking calming, coping thoughts.
- **d** Coming out of one's shell when calm and thinking of some solutions for the problem.

Teaching of the turtle technique can be enhanced by the use of a turtle puppet to demonstrate the technique and hold children's interest. Other activities can include having children make little cardboard turtles with heads that can be retracted into their shells, and using 'turtle tokens' to reward children who have coped well with a frustrating or disappointing situation. It is important to notice and reward successes as much as possible to assist children when things go wrong.

Effective use of the turtle technique (and other impulse control and anger management techniques for children) requires consistent reinforcement over time. If a child reacts angrily to a disappointment or playground contretemps, use the situation as an opportunity to remind him of the turtle technique, get the child to rehearse 'going into his shell', and then help him to generate some solutions.

## *Managing sadness & depression*

It is important to distinguish clearly between sadness and depression. Sadness is a healthy, adaptive response to loss, disappointment, or other negative experiences. Depression, although often used loosely to refer to a despondent mood, is an emotional disorder characterised by intense feelings of hopelessness, despair, guilt, loss of pleasure and interest in life, and other symptoms that impair a person's ability to function in the world. To qualify as a 'major depressive episode', symptoms need to persist for a period of two weeks. Due to significant changes in brain chemistry, depressed individuals cannot simply 'pull themselves together' or 'snap out of it'. Depression can occur in childhood and requires professional treatment, including possible pharmacotherapy. The strategies below for dealing with sadness are unlikely to be effective on their own to treat depression. However, they may be effective as part of a strategy to help 'prevent' depression.

## Talk about it

One of the most simple and effective means of coping with sadness is to talk about one's feelings with a person who is emotionally supportive, non-judgmental and caring. Encourage children to think of somebody whom they would trust enough to talk to if they felt really sad. A child who feels that there is nobody they could talk to is at risk. Try to connect such children to an appropriate adult support, such as a teacher, counsellor, or mentor.

## Draw it, paint it, dance it

One of the greatest psychological resources of childhood is play. Children have natural reserves of creativity that can be harnessed to help them process painful emotions. Provide opportunities for children to draw, write, paint, dance and play.

## Accept it

Remind children that sadness is normal, and that everyone feels blue from time to time. Remind them that they have felt sad in the past, and that it passed.

## Keep doing the things you enjoy

When one feels disheartened, it is easy to neglect the fun things one would do in a better mood. Social contact is particularly important.

## Exercise

Exercise is a natural anti-depressant. It produces endorphins, the natural 'happy hormones' of the brain, as well as promoting general physical and mental wellbeing.

## Challenge pessimism & 'catastrophising'

One can accept that one is feeling sad without necessarily accepting the gloomy, pessimistic thoughts that may accompany the mood. Gently challenge children's negative generalisations, such as, 'Nothing ever works out for me!', by saying something like, 'I know it feels like that right now, but that's not really true you know ...' Encourage them to acknowledge what they feel sad or disappointed about in the moment and express empathy, but do not go along with pessimistic generalisations. These have been shown to be associated with depression.

## Using Emotion Coaching to Develop Self-Regulation & Resilience

### *What is emotion coaching?*

Emotion coaching is helping children understand the different emotions they experience, why they occur, and how to handle them. In the simplest terms, we can coach children about emotions by comforting them, listening to and understanding their thoughts and feelings, and helping them understand themselves. As we do this, our children will feel loved, supported, respected and valued. With this emotionally supportive foundation, the adult will be much more successful at setting limits and problem-solving.

### *The benefits of emotion coaching*

In their paper published in 1996, Gottman, Katz & Hooven outlined different types of parental philosophies and approaches. These included an emotion-coaching philosophy and a dismissing meta-emotion philosophy. The emotion-coaching philosophy, in which the parents are comfortable with the emotions of themselves and their children, was seen to be the most helpful, and the emotion-dismissing philosophy in which parents view negative emotions as harmful was seen to be the most damaging.

In essence, the research shows that children raised by parents who value and guide emotions do better in many ways:

- They form stronger friendships.
- They perform better in school.
- They have fewer problems with negative emotions and are able to bounce back more quickly after a setback.
- They will get sick less often.

### *Learning how to emotion coach*

While emotion coaching may seem complicated at first, as we practise we find that it becomes second nature.

#### Step 1

Understand how *you* deal with feelings. Before you can become an emotion coach, you must first understand your own approach to emotions. Some parents, for example, are uncomfortable with their child's negative emotions. If a child feels sad, you might think that if you fix the problem that created the sadness, the sadness will go away. You might be uncomfortable with your own anger, because it makes you feel out of control, and in turn you discourage anger in your children.

Gottman suggests several questions you can ask yourself to discover why you feel the way you do about emotions:

1. Did your parents treat sad and angry moments as natural occurrences?
2. Did your parents lend an ear when family members felt unhappy, fearful, or angry?
3. Did your family use times of unhappiness, fear, or anger to show each other support, offer guidance, and help each other solve problems?
4. Was anger always viewed as potentially destructive? If so, what did this teach you about how to handle your anger? Are you taking this same approach with your children?
5. Was fear looked on as cowardly? If so, how did you learn to handle fear?
6. Was sadness seen as self-pity in your family? What ways were you taught to handle sadness?
7. Were sadness, anger and fear shoved under the carpet or dismissed as unproductive, frivolous, dangerous, or self-indulgent?

Research has shown that parents who have become good at emotion-coaching believe the following about emotions:

1. Their child's feelings are important.
2. Their child's feelings and wishes are okay, even if their actions are not.
3. Experiencing negative emotions, such as sadness, anger or fear, is important.
4. Negative feelings are a chance for parents and children to grow closer.
5. Understanding what causes their child's feelings is important.
6. Negative feelings are an opportunity for problem-solving.

## Step 2

Believe that the child's negative emotions are an opportunity for closeness and teaching. Reasoning away a child's emotion with logic rarely works. Parents who try to do this usually end up arguing with their child. Instead, a child's negative feelings are more likely to go away when children talk about them, label them, and feel understood. When children feel understood by their parents, they feel closer to them.

## Step 3

Listen with empathy and understanding, and then validate your child's feelings. Empathetic listeners do the following:

- Use their eyes to identify physical evidence of a child's emotions, such as a suddenly reduced appetite.
- Use their ears to hear the underlying messages behind what a child is saying.
- Use their imaginations to put themselves in a child's shoes to understand how they are feeling.
- Use words to reflect back what they hear, see, and imagine in a soothing, non-judgmental way. These words also help the child label the emotion.
- Use their hearts to feel what a child is feeling.

Once the child feels understood, let them know that their feelings and wishes are okay, even if their actions are not. The following tips will help you listen empathetically and validate the child's feelings:

1 Share simple observations. Say what you see and hear rather than ask probing questions. Children often do not know what they are feeling or why they are experiencing a feeling. For example, 6-year-old Elizabeth is much quieter than usual. She eats her afternoon snack with little enthusiasm before trudging off to her room. Her mother silently notices all this, and then makes the observation, 'Elizabeth, you seem quiet today.' When Elizabeth hardly responds, her mother offers a second observation: 'Often when I'm quiet, I'm worried about something.' Elizabeth then opens up to her mother and confides her worries about her friends who are being unkind to her at school.

2 Avoid questions you already know the answer to. When you ask questions such as, 'Who made the carpet dirty?' (knowing very well the answer), you create an environment of mistrust. Instead, be direct: 'You made the carpet dirty; I'm disappointed.'

3 Share examples from your own life. This helps children feel that what they are experiencing is normal.

## Step 4

Label the child's emotions. Children often do not know what they are feeling. If you label an action – observe aloud that they seem 'angry' or 'sad' or 'disappointed' – you can help the child transform a scary, uncomfortable feeling into something identifiable and normal. Researchers have shown that the simple act of labelling an emotion has a soothing effect on the nervous system, which helps children recover more quickly from an upsetting experience.

Often a chance to label an emotion comes up when you are listening empathetically. Keep in mind that it is easy to fall into the trap of telling your child how he *ought* to feel instead of *what* he's feeling. For example, 4-year-old Jared announces that he hates his friend Billy because Billy took his toy, then hit him when Jared tried to get his toy back. His mum, instead of telling Jared that he does not hate Billy and that he actually likes Billy because they are friends, says, 'It sounds like you are quite angry that Billy took your toy and hit you.'

## Step 5

Set limits, while exploring possible solutions to the problem that caused the negative emotion. There are several stages to this step:

1. Set limits. Even though it is important to validate the child's feelings, we do not have to validate their actions. Once we set a limit on inappropriate behaviour and its consequences, we can follow through and be consistent. The ideal time to use emotion coaching is right after the child misbehaves and before we present them with the consequences. For example, the adult might say, 'You're angry that Danny took that game away from you. I would be, too. But it's not okay for you to hit him. What can you do instead?'
2. Identify goals. After we have followed through on consequences for inappropriate behaviour, we can then identify the goal the child was trying to reach with his or her behaviour. Simply ask the child what he was trying to accomplish.
3. Think of possible solutions. Allow the child to think up solutions to a problem situation before you offer suggestions. This helps the child develop problem-solving skills. Do not shoot down his solutions if they are not workable. Instead, ask questions that will help him see the outcome of his solutions.
4. Evaluate the proposed solutions. When your child suggests solutions, ask questions like:
   - **i** Is this solution fair?
   - **ii** Will this solution work?
   - **iii** Is it safe?
   - **iv** How are you likely to feel? How are other people likely to feel?
5. Help the child choose a solution. If the child comes up with an unworkable solution, it is fine to go forward, as long as it is harmless. Let them learn from seeing the consequences of their

choices. Just leave the door open to rework the solution if it does not seem to be working. Also help the child come up with a plan of action to accomplish the solution.

## Developing a Growth Mindset in Young Children

The concept of 'mindset' is extremely important to us all, in that it underpins our overall wellbeing and impacts upon the ways in which we respond to stress and change in our lives. Our mindset will determine how we approach challenges and opportunities and it will also determine the world we encounter and possibilities we apprehend. Dweck (2007) distinguishes two extremes of the mindsets people tend to have about their basic qualities:

In a fixed mindset, your qualities are carved in stone. Ultimately, you believe that whatever skills, talents and capabilities you have are predetermined and finite. Whatever you lack, you will continue to lack. This fixed mindset applies not just to your own qualities, but to the qualities of others.

In a growth mindset, you believe your basic qualities are things you can cultivate through your efforts and everyone can change and grow through application and experience. Hard work really does result in good and positive outcomes. Qualities like intelligence are perceived to be a starting point, but success comes as a result of effort, learning and persistence.

### *The mindset paradox: the greatest threat to success is avoiding failure*

One of the most provocative aspects of Dweck's work is what it says about our approach to challenges. In a fixed mindset, people tend to avoid challenging situations that might lead to failure, because success depends upon protecting and promoting our set of fixed qualities and concealing our deficiencies. If we do fail, we focus on rationalising the failure, rather than learning from it and developing our capabilities. With a growth mindset, we focus on learning and development rather than failure and actively pursue the types of challenges that will probably lead to both learning and failure. It is therefore essential that, as adults who care for children and young people, we develop our own growth mindset in order to also model and support the development of this in our children.

### *Twenty-five ways to develop a growth mindset*

1. Acknowledge and embrace imperfections. Hiding from your weaknesses means you will never overcome them.
2. View challenges as opportunities. Having a growth mindset means relishing opportunities for self-improvement.

3 Try different learning tactics. There is no one-size-fits-all model for learning. What works for one person may not work for you.

4 Follow the research on brain plasticity. The brain is not fixed; the mind should not be either.

5 Replace the word 'failing' with the word 'learning'. When you make a mistake or fall short of a goal, you have not failed; you have learned.

6 Stop seeking approval. When you prioritise approval over learning, you sacrifice your own potential for growth.

7 Value the process over the end result. Intelligent people enjoy the learning process, and do not mind when it continues beyond an expected time frame.

8 Cultivate a sense of purpose. Dweck's research also showed that children with a growth mindset had a greater sense of purpose. Keep the big picture in mind.

9 Celebrate growth with others. If you truly appreciate growth, you will want to share your progress with others.

10 Emphasise growth over speed. Learning fast is not the same as learning well, and learning well sometimes requires allowing time for mistakes.

11 Reward actions, not traits. Tell children and young people when they are doing something smart, not just being smart.

12 Redefine 'genius'. The myth's been shattered: being a genius requires hard work – not simply talent.

13 Portray criticism as positive. You do not have to use that hackneyed term, 'constructive criticism', but you do have to believe in the concept.

14 Disassociate improvement from failure. Stop assuming that 'room for improvement' translates into failure.

15 Provide regular opportunities for reflection. Let children (and yourself) reflect on their learning at least once a day.

16 Place effort before talent. Hard work should always be rewarded before inherent skill.

17 Highlight the relationship between learning and 'brain training'. The brain needs to be 'worked out', just like the muscles of the body.

18 Cultivate grit. Children and young people with that extra bit of determination will be more likely to seek approval from themselves rather than others.

19 Abandon the image. 'Naturally smart' sounds just about as believable as 'spontaneous generation'. You will not achieve the image if you are not ready for the work.

**20** Use the word 'yet'. Dweck says 'not yet' has become one of her favourite phrases. Whenever you see children struggling with a task, just tell them they have not mastered it yet.

**21** Learn from other people's mistakes. It is not always wise to compare yourself to others, but it is important to realise that humans share the same weaknesses.

**22** Make a new goal after each goal is accomplished. You will never be able to stop learning. Just because your exam is over does not mean you should stop being interested in a subject. Growth-minded people know how to constantly create new goals to keep themselves stimulated.

**23** Take risks in the company of others. Stop trying to save face all the time and just allow yourself to get it wrong occasionally. It will make it easier to take risks in the future.

**24** Think realistically about time and effort. It takes time to learn. Do not expect to master every single topic in one go.

**25** Take ownership over your attitude. Once you develop a growth mindset, own it. Acknowledge yourself as someone who possesses a growth mentality and be proud to let it guide you throughout your life. As stated previously, it is so important for adults who are nurturing young children to not only understand this concept, but to also model the growth mindset in their own behaviours and interactions with the child.

## Building Confidence

Why is confidence important? When we have confidence in our abilities, it helps us to respond to problems with resilience. This 'I can do it' attitude motivates us to keep trying even when things are difficult. If we keep trying, our efforts are more likely to pay off and we feel a sense of accomplishment.

We start to develop confidence in our ability to make things happen very early in life. When babies cry and their parents respond, they begin to learn they have some control over their environment. They develop a sense of security and learn to trust that their parents will take care of their needs. As they grow, this security and trust allows children to feel safe enough to explore their environment. The enjoyment children get from exploring their world motivates them to 'master' the tasks that come with their age and stage. These accomplishments help children develop confidence in their ability to handle challenges and frustrating situations throughout their lives. Helping children gain confidence is best done in a caring relationship and is an important part of self-regulation.

Ways to develop confidence include the following:

- Encourage children to keep on trying even when the task is hard or frustrating. Give children the courage to keep going. 'That's it! You almost did it. Keep going … Good for you. You kept trying and you did it!'
- Show your children that 'Mistakes are okay'. People who believe that mistakes are a natural part of learning are more confident about trying new things. 'That's OK. We all make mistakes. It's how we learn. Now you know to do it differently the next time.'
- Be a 'Strengths Detective'. Pointing out your children's strengths is a much better confidence-builder than focusing on their limitations.
- Sometimes, if their behaviour is challenging, it may be hard to see a child's strengths. But all children have them. If we encourage activities that build on their strengths, it motivates them to develop interests they enjoy. When this happens, we often see an improvement in their behaviour.
- Give your children lots of time to just play. When children play they can take the time they need to master activities that interest them. This builds confidence and motivation to try new things. Playing also promotes development of flexible thinking and creative problem-solving skills.
- Set children up for success. Encourage them to do a task one step at a time. This helps children see their progress step-by-step and motivates them to keep trying. Give them things to do that they are capable of, but also challenge them to learn something new.
- Activities that gently stretch your children's abilities help them tolerate small amounts of 'healthy' stress. This shows them that effort is needed to learn new things and solve problems. It also helps them learn to deal with frustrations in daily life.
- Offer choices. Simple choices build children's confidence by giving them the chance to make decisions and have some control.
- Keep it simple. Offer only two or three choices so your children do not feel overwhelmed. 'Do you want to have a banana or a yogurt for snack?', or 'It's cold outside. Do you want to wear your hat or pull up your hood?'
- Encourage cooperation. Offer choices that encourage your children to do what you need them to do. Cooperation is more likely if they feel they have some control in the situation. For example, you can say, 'Dinner is ready. Do you want to wash your hands yourself? Or do you want my help?' Or: 'It's time for bed, do you want to walk up the stairs or do you want Daddy to carry you?'
- Keep safety in mind. For example, we do not give children a choice about wearing a seat belt, bike helmet, or holding hands when we cross a busy street.

- Encourage your children's positive choices. 'You made a good choice to put on your mittens. Now you can really play in the snow!', or 'You're getting along so well with your sister! It was a great choice to share the blocks.'
- Help your children be assertive. Children who stand up for themselves are less likely to be bullied. You can help your children set limits with their brothers, sisters, and friends by practising how to say 'No!', or 'I don't like that!', using an assertive voice and body language.
- Teach your children ways to solve problems and resolve conflicts. Help children 3 years and older identify the problem and think of positive solutions. 'There is a problem here because you both want to play with the yellow car. That's making you feel quite upset. Let's think of some ideas to solve the problem.' Then step back and let them try the solutions for themselves.
- Read or tell children stories about how others develop their strengths and confidence.

## Building Social Competence

Given the fact that social skills are clearly vital for a child's future development, it seems logical to ensure that such skills are taught within our school curriculum and fostered in the home context. The early years are when young children begin to develop these skills – learning to cooperate, take turns and solve the social problems that they are likely to encounter on a daily basis. Children need to learn how to wait their turn, share, resolve conflicts, cope effectively with anger, respond assertively in some contexts and gain confidence in social situations. If these skills are not learnt in the early years there will naturally be an impact upon overall development.

Children who have not been nurtured within secure contexts and have consequently not developed secure attachments will require additional support. This lack of nurture will have resulted in significant gaps in social, emotional and cognitive learning. Children need to progress through a series of developmental stages, one of which needs to involve exploratory play. Without this kind of natural progression they will fail to develop the social and emotional skills necessary to access an age-appropriate curriculum.

Children who have not had access to such environments need additional teaching to learn how to interact socially, ask for help and support, assert themselves and manage anxiety and stress. They also need to be provided with opportunities to learn these skills through play, as many of them will clearly have missed out on this particular stage and consequently find it difficult to interact appropriately and to engage in learning tasks.

## *The vicious cycle*

Children who present as aggressive – both physically and verbally – tend to be rejected by their peers, while those who present as withdrawn may often be left out of activities, isolated and ignored. As a consequence this can result in a vicious cycle in which these children do not interact as much as others in their peer group. They subsequently have fewer opportunities to learn, practise and develop the basic social skills that they need in order to become socially integrated. Such children will tend to fall behind socially and the gap between them and others in their peer group may well increase to a significant level. This is particularly distressing for all involved given the fact that these early years are so crucial in terms of social and emotional development.

## *Social skills reinforcement & generalisation in everyday situations*

The fact that young children learn best through modelling and practice is beyond question. We also know that social success is critical for broader success, and resilience research shows that children who are popular, likeable and able to resolve conflicts with others are also more likely to succeed at school, and are generally more resilient than children with less developed social skills. Social skills are complex and multi-faceted.

However, it is often assumed that social skills will be 'picked up' by osmosis. This is generally not the case, as while many social skills may be learned implicitly, all children can benefit from being taught social skills explicitly, not only those children who are developmentally lagging behind their peers.

The building blocks of social competence are as follows:

- Basic interaction skills (e.g., smiling, making eye contact, listening)
- Entry/approach skills (how to approach an individual socially or join a group)
- Maintenance skills (e.g., how to share, take turns, follow rules, cooperate etc.)
- Friendship skills (e.g., how to show appropriate affection, involve others in decision-making, be inclusive, etc.)
- Conflict resolution (how to manage disagreements in a socially acceptable manner)
- Empathy
- Communication of needs and ideas
- Sense of humour

- Assertiveness (how to say no to engaging in dangerous or antisocial behaviour, stand up for oneself, etc.)

## Ages & stages of social development

The following guide shows social skills development appropriate to various ages. However, it should be borne in mind that there is no universal developmental timetable. Also, many of the skills listed below are more like works in progress than milestones of achievement; they develop slowly over years, gradually becoming more sophisticated and well-established.

| Age | Social behaviours |
|---|---|
| 2 | Social awareness is very limited. Play tends to be solitary, although toddlers will closely observe and copy adults and other children. Direct interaction is minimal, apart from squabbles over toys! |
| 3 | Parallel play develops: children play alongside one another, with some interaction.<br>Beginning to learn to share and take turns.<br>Beginning to learn to manage physical aggression. |
| 4–5 | Cooperative play develops. Children start to play group games. Games become more complex and organised.<br>'Special' friendships begin to form.<br>Learning how to play fairly and abide by rules.<br>Can approach others and ask to join in with groups.<br>Begins to learn to be assertive and to ask others to stop if they are being annoying. |
| 6–8 | Learning to be a 'good winner' and a 'good loser'.<br>Can empathise with others in distress and offer appropriate support.<br>Learning to give and receive compliments from others.<br>Conversation skills developing: how to listen to others and take turns talking, etc.<br>Can ask an adult for support when needed.<br>Negotiation skills: including others in decision-making, learning to decide together and make suggestions rather than boss others around.<br>Able to say 'no' to peers when appropriate. |
| 9–12 | Learning to speak confidently in front of a group.<br>Learning to respect the opinions of others. |

## *Teaching social skills to children*

The following are some tips on how to teach social skills to children, both at school and in the home.

### Provide explicit instructions

Children often need to be given direct, explicit instructions about how to behave in specific social situations. For example, a child may need to be told that it is important to say 'hello' back when somebody greets them, or to smile when approaching a child to ask to join in a game. Of course, this kind of instruction is provided all of the time by parents and teachers who remind children to say 'thank you', or not to interrupt when someone else is talking. However, there are often significant gaps in this instruction. For example, while most children are instructed to say 'please' and 'thank you', fewer are explicitly told how to be a 'good sport' (Do not comment on another player's poor moves or bad luck. Do not taunt someone for losing. Accept bad luck without complaining, etc.). Learning these skills is not easy, and most children will need to be told the same information many times before they learn it fully.

### Provide structured learning opportunities

Social skills cannot be taught by instruction alone. Children need ample social opportunities to develop their skills. Whilst there are numerous social opportunities at school, most of the time social interaction is unstructured. Children with good social skills therefore tend to get many opportunities to reinforce their skills, while more shy or aggressive children often have fewer chances to learn, thus creating a growing gap between socially skilled and unskilled children. The following are some examples of simple, structured activities which teach social skills:

- To teach sharing, set up a cooperative activity in which children have to share a limited set of resources.
- To teach fair play, provide instructions on how to play fairly, then get children to play a game (e.g., snakes and ladders), during which children can be reminded of the rules. Rewards can be provided to those who played well.
- Use role-plays to practise various skills, such as ignoring a person who is teasing you, or approaching a group or person to ask to join a game.

When children experience social problems, such as conflict with a friend, or rejection by a group, it is often tempting for parents to jump in and try to solve the problem for them. However, except in situations involving bullying or other unacceptable behaviour, it is generally better to assist children to solve their own social problems rather than intervening directly. This can be done by asking children to think of ways that they might be able to deal with the situation, providing feedback on their ideas, and perhaps offering some suggestions, then encouraging them to try out the best options. In this way, children can learn a sense of social mastery through finding that they can deal with a difficult situation without direct adult help.

## Provide feedback.

Children are not always aware of the connection between their own behaviour and its social consequences. For example, a child who hits other children is likely to soon find themselves lacking in friends, yet may not necessarily understand why. Adults can help children to learn to connect their own behaviour with its results. Otherwise, children will tend to see their social experiences as having to do with who they are rather than how they behave. So, the child who hits out at others when upset is likely to feel that he or she is inherently unlikeable, rather than recognising that different behaviour might lead to a different result. Adults can help children to make these connections by asking, for example: 'How do you think so-and-so felt when you hit him? Do you think it's possible he might be feeling a bit scared that you are going to do that again?'.

## Effective Thinking

Cognitive Behaviour Therapy (CBT) shows us the role that thoughts play in relation to both our emotions and our behaviours and is probably the most helpful set of tools that we have in order to support the development of more effective thinking in our children and young people.

This approach focuses on the role that thoughts play in regard to both emotions and behaviour, and advocates that change in thought processes can have a significant effect upon altering behaviours. We all know that sometimes our children and young people can be consumed with anxious and negative thoughts and doubts. These messages will often reinforce a state of inadequacy and/or low levels of self-esteem.

The process of CBT helps to support them in reconsidering these negative assumptions. It also allows them to *learn how* to change their self-perceptions in order to improve their mental and emotional state – this is the key aim of this kind of approach. Changing negative thought patterns or opinions will ultimately help children and young people to become more able to control and change their behaviours, but this does take practice.

## *ABC*

The CBT approach breaks a particular problem into three smaller parts:

- **A**, the **activating event**, is often referred to as the 'trigger' – the thing that causes you to engage in the negative thinking.
- **B** represents these negative **beliefs**, which can include thoughts, rules and demands, and the meanings the individual attaches to both external and internal events.
- **C**, the **consequences**, or emotions, and the behaviours and physical sensations accompanying these different emotions. It is important to highlight and discuss with children how the way that they think about a problem can affect how they feel physically and emotionally. It can also alter what they do about it. This is why the key aim for CBT is to break the negative, vicious cycle that some children and young people may find themselves in. For example, if you think that you will get your work wrong, you feel angry and then you do not give it a try in case it is wrong.

When working with children and young people in identifying such faulty thinking, the main aim is to encourage them to break the negative cycle.

## *Strategies to help children & young people engage in more effective thinking*

The following key strategies are helpful to break this negative cycle and can be adapted/ differentiated for children and young people at each stage of development.

### Test the evidence

One of the most helpful interventions for developing new and more positive belief systems and for challenging these 'negative automatic thoughts' (NATs) is to test the evidence. Children can engage in the following questioning process:

1. What is the evidence for this thought?
2. What is the evidence against this thought?
3. What would my best friend say if they heard my thought?
4. What would my teacher say if he heard my thought?
5. What would my parents or carers say if they heard my thought?
6. What would I say to my best friend if they had this same thought?
7. Am I making mistakes? For example, blowing it up, forgetting my strengths or good points, self-blaming, predicting failure, or thinking that I can mind read what others are thinking?

This kind of strategy is particularly useful in terms of reinforcing the need to gather accurate evidence. What we believe about ourselves is not always true. It is not how others always see us and these kinds of beliefs need to be challenged in this way. Using this sort of questioning process, and gathering evidence in the form of such a behavioural experiment, is a particularly positive strategy for beginning to identify and challenge unhelpful beliefs that children may hold.

## Reframing

Negative thoughts can be reframed into more positive, balanced and realistic ones through 'reframing'. For example, 'I am just fat', could be reframed as, 'I need to lose some weight and tone up a bit, but my overall shape isn't that bad.' Or, 'I always get the maths work wrong', could be reframed as, 'Some of these sums are difficult, but I know I can do the basics – I just need to work hard and find help in order to improve my skills.'

## Distraction

Children can be encouraged to control their thoughts by thinking of something else:

- They can describe in detail what they see around them in order to feel calmer. They can attempt to name all of their favourite bands.
- They can use self-talk techniques and repeat a positive coping message until the negative automatic thought has gone.
- They can 'bin' the thoughts by writing them down and then screwing them up and putting them into the bin – symbolically eradicating these negative thoughts.
- Students can also keep a positive diary in order to record 'positive automatic thoughts' (PATs) that may occur during the day and engage in realistic goal-setting, which involves practice.

Overall, what is important when children and young people are engaged in learning and developing these skills is for adults to encourage them to set appropriate targets. Young people need to be reminded that we do not move forwards unless we set realistic goals for ourselves. These should be broken down into small, achievable steps and the ultimate goal continually focused upon. Setting targets allows us to visualise where we want to be in the future: if we feel that we have nowhere to go, and nothing to move towards, then ultimately we will not be able to effect the change necessary.

## Problem-Solving

We know that preschool children learn best from the everyday experience of solving problems that are meaningful to them. As a teacher or parent, it is helpful to observe those moments when children have problems and help them think about ways to solve their own problems. Anticipate problems before they escalate and help children identify possible solutions.

- Introduce a problem-solving procedure by teaching children the steps to solve social problems: 1) Identify what the problem is; 2) Think about solutions; 3) Think about what will happen if I do this and how the other child will feel if I do this?; and 4) Try the solution. You may want to teach the problem-solving steps by role-playing different scenarios throughout the day. This will help children understand and use this process. Hang the problem-solving steps at the children's eye level and refer to the steps frequently during daily interactions.
- During everyday conversations/talk times use puppets or toys to act out problem scenarios, for example, a situation in which one puppet does not share their toys. After that, talk with the children about how the puppets could solve their problem. As children come up with solutions, write them down. Talk with the children about which solutions will work and which are fair, and so on. Talk about the solutions as a group, have the pictures available to look at while children are solving real problems, and praise children for using solutions.
- Read stories about friendship skills. Talk about the characters' emotions and how the characters handle social situations.

### *The problem-solving process*

Problem-solving can be broken down into a four-step process that can be applied to almost any type of problem, from the social to the scientific:

1. Identify the problem
2. Generate solutions
3. Evaluate the possible solutions, decide on the best course of action, and put it into action
4. Evaluate the outcome. If the problem is not solved, repeat from step 2.

### Identify the problem

This step may sound obvious, but sometimes identifying the problem can be more difficult than it appears. Once the problem is clearly identified, this often goes more than halfway to solving it. Identifying the problem means clearly working out what one's goal is, and what is currently preventing one from achieving this outcome.

## Generate solutions

The key at this stage of the process is not to be overly critical or evaluative of the solutions generated, but to simply think of as many different ways of solving or addressing the problem as possible. This is a 'brainstorming' session. You get more creative solutions if you feel free to table anything.

## Evaluate solutions & choose the best one to act on

Having generated a list of possible approaches to dealing with the problem, it is now necessary to evaluate each of the options and decide on the preferred approach, taking into consideration everything that might be relevant to the decision. One's knowledge is rarely perfect, so this is a matter of a 'best guess' in most cases.

## Evaluate the outcome

Having tried a solution, it is important to evaluate the success of the solution. If it has not worked, return to step 2, and revisit the possible solutions. Continue this process until the problem is resolved.

## *Teaching the problem-solving process to children*

Children who are old enough to think abstractly (from around 12) can be taught the problem-solving process directly, using real-life examples and 'live applications' to illustrate the process. Younger children will learn best by having the process demonstrated repeatedly by adults to help them solve their day-to-day social and other problems.

For example, let us say two 5-year-old children are having a conflict in the playground. You can begin the problem-solving process by getting each child to clearly explain the problem (step one). Having found out that the problem centres on who will play Batman and who will play Robin in a game, you can ask the children to think of some solutions to the problem (step 2). If they are unable to come up with any ideas, you can offer some ideas, such as swapping roles at some point in the game, playing a different game in which they both can agree on the roles to be played, and so on. Once a solution has been agreed on by both children, the solution can be tried (step 3). Later you can ask the children how the solution worked, or, if you notice that the children are fighting again, you can assist them again by helping them think of some new alternatives (step 4).

In demonstrating problem-solving, adults should encourage children to generate solutions for themselves, rather than imposing their own 'best solution', however obvious it may appear to the adult. This allows children to practise thinking creatively about solutions to their problems rather than relying on adults to be there to sort everything out.

## Relax & Unwind

Both adults and children will need to develop the ability to relax and unwind in order to manage the everyday stresses they experience in their lives. In recent years, Mindfulness approaches have become increasingly popular as a means of supporting the development of such skills.

What is Mindfulness? Mindfulness is 'Paying attention on purpose, without judgement to our experience as it unfolds moment by moment' (Jon Kabat-Zinn, 1990, p.3). Mindfulness involves paying attention to the stream of consciousness of your mind, without judging it or changing it. This naturally quietens the mind and offers insights into the automatic habit-driven behaviours we develop in our lives. Left to itself the mind wanders through all kinds of thoughts, and mostly these thoughts are about the past or future. The past, however, no longer exists and the future has not yet arrived. The one moment we can actual experience – the present moment- is the one we often seem to avoid most. So, in mindfulness we are concerned with noticing what's going on right now, and this helps us to be fully 'awake' in our own lives. It is about noticing the little things on an ordinary day, and allowing ourselves just to 'be'.

There are significant health benefits to practising Mindfulness, as well as improving life satisfaction. Mindfulness regulates the stress response by strengthening the 'noticing' or 'thinking' part of the brain in the frontal lobes. It engages the parts of the brain that help to regulate emotions and create a sense of safety. Mindfulness helps all of the brain to work together as an integrated whole. The more you practise Mindfulness, the more your brain will remember to engage all of its parts, even in stressful situations. Mindfulness calms the amygdala, which is the 'smoke alarm' of the brain. Mindfulness has been shown to:

- Decrease stress, anxiety and depression
- Allow connection with the self and values
- Bring a sense of peacefulness and clarity
- Increase self-awareness
- Develop self-acceptance and confidence
- Bring emotional balance and stability
- Decrease worrying thoughts
- Allow compassion and empathy to grow

- Help to view experiences positively
- Improve sleep
- Strengthen the immune system and improve health
- Dramatically improve concentration and memory

## *Mindfulness in the home*

Mindfulness is a powerful life skill that can build psychological resilience. It is best taught to children from an early age, and the implementation of simple Mindfulness practices and routines can be of great value to children. Being Mindful in everyday life can be encouraged through simple activities such as cooking, eating and helping in the garden. Children will benefit through increased focus and attention, as well as learning to calm and lessen their own anxiety and stress.

Simple activities to promote Mindfulness include: jigsaws; concentration games; colouring in grids/mazes; periods of stillness; art and craft activities; nature walks; listening to music; mindful eating; finding an intensely pleasurable leisure activity, such as drawing, running, football, modelling.

Simple mindful relaxation activities for young children include the following:

### Best breathing!

Find a comfortable place to sit, with your eyes closed and your spine as straight as you can make it. Focus your attention on your breathing. When a thought or emotion pops into your head, accept it, but allow it to float on by (imagine you are pinning it to a cloud or onto a leaf floating down the river). Focus your attention on the rise and fall of your chest, the feeling of the air entering and leaving your body.

### The raisin exercise

Take a raisin and hold it in your hand. Look at it carefully, as if you are going to describe it to a Martian who has never seen one before. As best you can, be aware of thoughts or images that may sneak in as you look at this object. Simply note that they are just thoughts and return your attention to this object. Notice the colours of the object. What does the surface look like? Is it bumpy or smooth? Explore the object with your eyes and fingers. Is it dry or moist? Notice how the light shines on the object. Bring the raisin to your nose. Does it have any smell? Explore with your eyes, your fingers, and your nose. Is your attention on this raisin in your hand? Then, whenever you are ready, place the raisin in your mouth. Explore the object.

Do you notice your mouth watering? As best you can, keep your attention on the raisin and also watch your thoughts. Are the thoughts looking forward to swallowing the raisin and eating another, or are they attending to the sensations of the one that is in your mouth? Gently bite the raisin. Taste the flavour. Slowly chew the raisin while noting every sensation. As you swallow the raisin, first note the intention to swallow it. Then feel it slide down your throat and into your tummy. Can you feel that your body is now exactly one raisin heavier than it was a few minutes ago?

### Sunshine relaxation

Close your eyes ... be very still and imagine you are lying down outside in the warm sunshine. Your body feels totally relaxed and calm. As you lie comfortably in the soft grass, the rays of the sun are soaking into your muscles ... warming and relaxing your whole body. You can feel the warmth of the sun on your legs ... and then let them relax. Let the muscles around your tummy relax. Feel the sun's rays on your shoulders and arms as you relax into the carpet of grass. Now feel the warm sun on your face and ... as the sun touches it, your whole face relaxes. Relax your forehead, your cheeks, your eyes and your mouth ... relax, relax, relax.

## Encouraging Optimism

Optimism is often defined as a disposition to expect the best and view events and situations in a positive light. In the context of resilience, optimism refers to a sense of a positive future, to a tendency to find positive meaning in experiences, and a belief in one's ability to impact positively on one's environment and situation. Optimism has many benefits for mental health, including protecting against depression and anxiety. It also increases the likelihood of effective problem-solving. This is why it is vital to encourage the development of optimism in children and young people.

### *Aspects of optimism*

### Hopefulness, anticipation & a sense of a compelling future

These are key aspects of optimism. Children and young people who cannot envisage a bright future for themselves, or who believe that the world is hostile or indifferent to them, are vulnerable to depression, anxiety and despair.

## Orientation to future, goal directedness

Optimists are oriented towards a future in which they have clear goals that they look forward to fulfilling. Resilient children have been shown to have future plans that are realistic, positive and achievable. They tend to be oriented towards achievement, and have educational aspirations.

## Cognitive factors

Optimism can be seen as a way of processing information about the world that places an emphasis on the positive elements of experience. There are several aspects to the optimistic processing style:

1 **Maintaining perspective.** Optimists are able to step back from their problems and evaluate them in a wider context. They do not 'catastrophise' events by always imagining the worst possible outcome. They can see that everything changes, and bad times will pass.

2 **A belief in the ability to solve problems.** Optimists do not feel helpless in the face of life's difficulties, but have the ability to solve problems by rationally thinking through alternatives, evaluating them, and acting appropriately. Without the cognitive ability to problem-solve, it is easy for children and young people to feel overwhelmed by events that seems out of their control.

3. **Explanatory style.** Optimists and pessimists have different ways of explaining life's ups and downs to themselves. These differences are explained below.

## Sense of coherence & predictability in life

Children who have experienced many upheavals and changes in their lives, particularly those who have had major disruptions in their relationships with caregivers, may come to see life as unpredictable, random and untrustworthy. This lack of a sense of coherence threatens their capacity to develop healthy optimism. If nothing in life is stable, how is it possible to sustain a sense of trust in the processes of life, or to believe that one can effect positive change through one's own efforts? Whilst children can be taught the cognitive skills that underpin optimism, the sense of coherence and predictability engendered by stable relationships with caring adults and the presence of everyday routines and consistent boundaries is essential for the development of resilience.

### *Teaching optimism to children*

Some children tend to be naturally optimistic and persistent in the face of obstacles. Others are more sensitive to setbacks and prone to taking things badly. However, optimism is a learnable skill. Even adults with habitually very pessimistic ways of thinking can learn to think more optimistically. Children can learn optimism unconsciously by observing people around them, such as their parents. However, they can also be taught optimism explicitly, like any other skill. There are several steps to this process:

1. Helping children to realise that their feelings and responses to events are not caused just by the events themselves, but also by the way they think about these events (their 'self-talk').
2. Helping children to practise identifying their self-talk in different situations in their own lives.
3. Helping children to identify their own explanatory version of events and then challenging the accuracy of their beliefs.
4. Helping children to generate alternative, more optimistic explanations for the same events.

Children can also be taught to keep negative events in perspective through a process of examining their 'what-next' beliefs. This involves:

1. Assisting children to look at the best and worst possible outcomes of an event, and estimate the likelihood of each. This process is used to help them to arrive at a 'most likely' outcome.
2. Helping children to develop the problem-solving skills they need to deal with the most likely outcome.

Optimism can also be taught in less formal ways by teachers, parents, and others who have contact with children:

## Challenge pessimistic thinking

Notice when children make pessimistic pronouncements and challenge their assumptions. For example, if a child who has done poorly in a subject at school declares that they are 'just no good' at that subject, you can offer alternative ways of looking at the situation: perhaps they did not pay attention in class, or spend enough time on their homework?

## Provide encouragement

Help children to develop persistence and optimism in the face of setbacks by providing encouragement and support along the way. Children do not always have the 'built-in' persistence they need in order to succeed. However, if they are consistently provided with encouragement and support from adults, they will eventually internalise this support and develop the capacity to persevere on their own.

### Model optimistic thinking

Children learn from observing others. If you express optimism, perseverance and resilience in the face of day-to-day obstacles, your children will learn by example. If you notice that you tend towards pessimism, start working on your own thinking.

### Use stories promoting persistence & optimism

Children learn through stories. When children are confronted with a difficult situation in their lives, you can tell stories from your own life that emphasise how you got through a hard time or succeeded despite an initial failure. Books and films that have an optimistic message can also be helpful.

### Emphasise strengths & acknowledge successes

Consistently acknowledge children's efforts and successes. When children do not succeed, emphasise the positive aspects of the situation, for example, how proud you are of the effort they put in. Do not, however, reward poor efforts with praise.

### Teach problem-solving

When children feel overwhelmed or anxious about a situation, help them to learn problem-solving skills by asking them to think about a number of alternatives for dealing with the problem. Do not step in to solve the problem for them.

### Set high, but realistic standards

It is important that the standards set for children are high, but achievable. High standards encourage children to reach their potential and strive to go beyond themselves. Of course, setting impossible standards will only dishearten children, so expectations need to be realistic.

## Planning for Transition & Change

We live in a constantly changing world. The pace of change is more rapid than it has ever been. New products and processes are continually available and the speed at which we are exposed to new information is continually increasing. This can be overwhelming at times. Sometimes we are able to shelter our children from so much change, but often not. If it is overwhelming to us, how does it feel to children? And that is just 'normal', everyday change. What about the big unexpected changes?

Most of us, and especially children, appreciate some level of 'sameness' in our lives. That does not mean that we do not appreciate the new and the novel, but we tend to prefer sameness to change. Children need time to process all of the information that they are exposed to and appreciate daily routines and repetition, or they may become stressed. They like knowing that when they arrive home from school they will play and then have dinner, and then there is a bath and then two stories. Children thrive on the predictability of daily routines. So, helping them to cope with both little and big changes is really essential.

## *Tips for helping children cope with major changes*

- **Give advance warning.** Have a discussion, for example: 'The place where Mum works thinks she will be a bigger help if we move to another place. We are going to look for a new house in a place called Bristol. Will you help us choose the new house?'
- **Keep as much the same as possible.** During a big change, such as adding a sibling to the family, try to keep as much the same as possible. For example, this is not the best time to also move the child from a cot to big bed.
- **Answer all their questions.** Depending on the child's age, they may have a lot of questions. Do your best to answer them all, even if some are repeated many times.
- **Expect that some regression may happen.** At times of change children may regress to earlier behaviours. For example, a child who was toilet-trained may revert back to having accidents. This is normal – strive for patience.
- **Be accepting of grieving.** Your child may go through a process that looks a lot like grieving as they navigate new waters with a new house, sibling, teacher or school. Listen, do not be too quick to distract and, at the end, remind them of all the positives.

During times of change, a little extra attention will go a long way in helping children deal with stress. Plan an hour or a half hour each week during which the child has your undivided attention. It is important to use play to aid your child's development. Let the child pick the activity or follow their lead. For example, if the child wants to drop a toy over and over again from their high chair, retrieve the toy and let them drop it again. Or if the child wants to make a cake, find time to do that and let them take an active role in the process, even if they make a mess. How does that help the child deal with change? Extra attention and patience from us, as adults, helps our children understand that although some aspects of life are changing, our love and care will remain constant.

## Strategies for supporting young children to manage change in daily life

**1** Break it down

Do a task analysis to break the transition into smaller steps, so you can identify where the problem is. Moving from computer time to another activity provides an example:

| Step | Possible Issues |
|---|---|
| 1. Playing computer game | Does it make him feel frustrated? Happy? Over-excited? |
| 2. Computer time is over | How does he know? Does he get any warning? |
| 3. Leaving the computer | Is the game still running? Is there a routine for leaving? |
| 4. Moving to the next activity | Does he know where to go? Can he still hear the game? |
| 5. Starting the next activity | Does he know what to do? Does he have what he needs? |

**2** Show that change can be fun

Use two activities that the child loves equally and practise switching between them. Teach them to recognise what a transition is, when it is coming and how it will feel. Make it a rewarding, stress-free time so they can focus on learning the cues and experiencing the change as a pleasant thing.

**3** Ease into it

Sometimes making a transition less obvious by blurring the lines between activities, or making the steps between them smaller, can help close a gap that feels too intimidating to cross. Let the child bring toys from the floor to the kitchen table while you make breakfast, then put them away when their cereal is ready.

**4** Be prepared

The best way to cope with transitions is to know that they are coming. Get into the habit of thinking about the plan for the day, the week, the month ahead and identify times of transition in advance.

**5** Use a schedule

This is one of the most important tools for helping younger children to deal with change. Listing the activities for the day will help the child to know what to expect, show the sequence of events and highlight times of transition.

**6** Make the end obvious

Moving on to a new activity is difficult if you do not realise that the old one is finished. Find ways to make it clear when a task is over – pull the picture from the schedule and put it in a 'completed' basket, or have photos of what the finished task looks like.

**7** Use transition cues

Give plenty of warning that a change is coming, using tangible signals that are clear, obvious and unique to each transition – play Bob the Builder theme music when it is time to pack up the toys, for example.

**8** Use a timer

Time is a really abstract concept, so translating it into something visual will help signal that a transition is coming up. The best 'timers' show time passing in some concrete way, such as an egg timer, where time 'disappears' with the countdown to a transition.

**9** Define physical areas and boundaries

Moving between tasks becomes easier when it is clear where to go and what to do there – mark a spot on the floor for the child to sit at mat time, or show them on a map the spots where they can play during lunchtime.

**10** Teach transition words

Before you can start to communicate with young children about transitioning, they need to understand concepts like 'first', 'then', 'after', 'next', 'now' and 'later'. Use the words often and play simple games to reinforce these ideas.

- First you roll the ball to me, then I roll it back to you.
- Now we're watching Thomas, after we'll bake the biscuits.
- Your brother is first in the bath and then you're next.
- You can have a drink after you wash your hands.
- Let's line up the toys … Teddy is first, Nemo is next, Spiderman is last.

# Part 2
# Activities

1 Finding My Strengths

2 Worry Warrior

3 Relaxation Tools

4 Visualisation

5 Face Your Fears

6 Anger Antics

7 Thought Bubbles

8 I Can't Do It … Yet!

9 A Good Mistake

10 My Feelings

11 My Day

12 The Problem-Solving Tree & Flower

13 Goals Rocket & Overcoming Your Gremlins

14 My Mountain

15 Mood Marbles

16 Stop & Think about the Good Times!

17 Magic Circles

18 Oops!

19 Magic Language

20 What Lit the Fuse?

21 My Good Deeds Ladder

22 Mindful Moments

23 What's in the Box?

24 Using Grit

25 Fantasy Island

26 All about Me

27 Bottling Thoughts

28 Helping Hand

29 Problem-Solving

30 My Strengths & Skills

# The Activities

The activities in this section have been written for flexible use with individual children, small groups and whole classes of young children. They can be used as stand-alone activities or as a block, as needed.

Details of how to use the activities with different groups are provided in the text of the activities, including suggested extensions to activities, if this seems appropriate.

## Overview of Activities

1 **Finding My Strengths.** Making choices and identifying personal strengths; for use with individuals or small groups.

2 **Worry Warrior.** Only for children who worry excessively; for individuals, or small groups.

3 **Relaxation Tools.** For use with individuals, small groups, or in a whole class.

4 **Visualisation.** For use with individuals, small groups, or in a whole class.

5 **Face Your Fears.** Only for children suffering excessive fears and as a one-to-one activity.

6 **Anger Antics.** Only for children experiencing excessive anger issues and as a one-to-one activity.

7 **Thought Bubbles.** Children with reasonable language and attention skills and some self-awareness can engage in this activity; for use with individuals or small groups.

8 **I Can't Do It … Yet!** Focusing on the value of persistence and determination; for use with individuals, small groups, or whole classes.

9 **A Good Mistake.** A story that provokes reflection and discussion on the value of 'failing' and making mistakes; for use with individuals, small groups, or whole classes.

10 **My Feelings.** For children old enough to understand the concept and vocabulary of emotions; individuals, small groups, or whole classes.

11 **My Day.** Children are encouraged to record and reflect on what has happened during their day; for use with individuals, small groups, or whole classes.

12 **The Problem-Solving Tree & Flower.** Supporting the acquisition of problem-solving skills; for use with individuals, small groups, or whole classes.

13 **Goals Rocket & Overcoming your Gremlins.** Focusing on personal determination, the acquisition of problem-solving skills and an understanding of how worry may hold us back. This is best used with individuals who are struggling with worries.

14 **My Mountain.** Supporting determination and the acquisition of problem-solving skills; for use with individuals, small groups, or whole classes.

15 **Mood Marbles.** Introduces a method of reflecting on and recording feelings; for use with individuals, small groups, or whole classes.

16 **Stop & Think about the Good Times!** An activity focused on increasing our awareness of thought processes; for use with individuals, small groups, or whole classes.

17 **Magic Circles.** This activity supports a change in focus to positive, rather than negative, events; for use with individuals, small groups, or whole classes.

18 **Oops!** For children struggling to maintain a positive outlook. For use only with individuals, after they have completed Activity 17.

19 **Magic Language.** This is an activity based on the adult facilitator's modelling of assertive and positive language; for use with individuals, small groups, or whole classes.

20 **What Lit the Fuse?** For children struggling with excessive anger; individuals or very small groups.

21 **My Good Deeds Ladder.** Each person creates a record of their 'good deeds'; for use in small groups, or as a whole class.

22 **Mindful Moments.** Mindfulness practices for regular use with individuals or in a group.

23 **What's in the Box?** This is a turn-taking game for two to four children, plus two adults.

24 **Using Grit.** This includes some ideas for developing 'grit' and personal determination; for individuals or larger groups.

25 **Fantasy Island.** A useful 'getting to know you' exercise, for individuals or larger groups.

26 **All About Me.** A useful 'getting to know you' exercise, for individuals or larger groups.

27 **Bottling Thoughts.** For children who have some understanding of how our thoughts affect us; best with individuals. There is an activity extension included for children who are excessively worried.

28 **Helping Hand.** Children are asked to reflect on their own personal strengths and supportive people in their lives; for use in small groups, or as a whole class.

29 **Problem-Solving.** This activity provides a practical problem-solving tool; best done only with individuals.

30 **My Strengths & Skills.** For use with one, target, child. This activity involves three to five adults or children over 8 years old, plus the child who is the focus of the activity. The target child should be able to listen for at least 2 minutes.

# Activity 1
# Finding My Strengths

 Individuals  Small groups

## Aims

To identify personal strengths and preferences in a fun and active way.

## Materials

Two boxes to hold a range of small items that take into account the interests of the individual or group. For example: carrot, doll, fancy dress hat, musical instrument, ball, piece of pasta, plastic snow globe, pencil, toy magic wand, a leaf, a soft blanket, apple, toy car, fancy dress hat, musical instrument, teddy, puzzle piece, paintbrush, sports shoe, toy food, a pair of wellies, piece of tin foil. A set of laminated Choices Cards (Worksheet 1, 'Choices Cards'), instant-print camera, blindfolds & folders (one of each, per person). Extension: Worksheet 2, 'My Skills & Strengths', pencils or pens.

## Activity

Prepare the two boxes, dividing the set of Choices Cards and the small items equally between the two boxes; make sure there are the same number of items in each box and that no item is repeated. Prepare a personal tray for each child by taking their photograph and fixing it to their own tray.

This activity should be modelled by two adults, or an adult and a child before moving around the group. Wearing a blindfold, the children take it in turns to pick two items out, one from each box (if they do not want to wear a blindfold that is fine, but it can add to the fun and the mystery).

When they have picked their two items they open their eyes and are asked: 'Which One?' Whichever they pick goes into their tray. When they have six items in their tray, take a photograph of the items for their folders.

*Page 1 of 2*

Now use the 'Which One?' question again, a few times, to narrow down their choices to their three favourite things, strengths, or activities. Take another photograph and label it 'My Top Three'.

## Extension

If children's language is good enough and if they are motivated to do so, help them reflect on their strengths by asking them about their top three. Why these three? What do they tell me about you? What are you good at? If appropriate try Worksheet 2, 'My Skills & Strengths'. If necessary, the facilitator can help to write or illustrate the responses.

# Worksheet 1
## Choices Cards

| | |
|---|---|
| Music | Talking |
| Active | Reading |
| Quiet | Listening |
| Imagination | Sports |
| Drawing | Helping |
| Sorting | Building |
| Counting | Running |

# Worksheet 2

# My Skills & Strengths

| Things I am good at ... | How I could use this? |
|---|---|
| ◆ ______________________ | ◆ ______________________ |
| ◆ ______________________ | ◆ ______________________ |
| ◆ ______________________ | ◆ ______________________ |
| ◆ ______________________ | ◆ ______________________ |
| ◆ ______________________ | ◆ ______________________ |
| ◆ ______________________ | ◆ ______________________ |
| ◆ ______________________ | ◆ ______________________ |

Think ahead!  Use your skills!

# Activity 2
# Worry Warrior

  Small groups

## Aims

This activity is for children who seem to be worrying about things. If a child seems not to be worried, do not use this activity as we do not want them to start thinking that they should be worrying! The activity aims to identify worries and offer solutions.

## Materials

Story books (see below); paper & stiff card, pens, coloured pencils & felt-tip pens, scissors; shoe boxes or similar for the 'worry boxes', craft materials (glue, glitter, pieces of fabric, etc.).

## Activity

Write out the text for 'Naming the Worry' (see below) on small slips of paper in advance; cut up at least three small pieces of blank card per child for each person to write their worries on.

At the beginning of the session, do *not* say, 'We will be looking at worries.' Instead, introduce the word 'worry' and the concepts of being worried and not worried through a story. Read the story a few times over the course of a few days to a week. The story should be matched to the language level, interests and worries of the individual or group. Here is a selection that could be used (full references in 'Recommended Reading & Resources for Parents, Carers & Professionals):

- *Do Not Feed the Worry Bug* (Green, 2011)
- *Charley Chatty & the Wiggly Worry Worm* (Naish, Jefferies & Farrell, 2016)
- *But What If? A book about feeling worried* (Graves & Guicciardini, 2013)

Now follow the lead of the child or group by having an open discussion of the story. What did they like and not like about it? Who was their favourite character and why? What was the story about? Do they ever feel like anyone in the story felt? Did they notice the word 'worry' in the story? What does it mean to them? What kinds of things do people worry about and why? What kinds of things do you worry about and why? What can people do to feel less worried?

Next do a brainstorm about what worries *feel* like (e.g., a wiggly worm, a fire-breathing monster, space in my tummy, etc.). This could include drawing. Noticing a worried feeling and describing it or drawing it is a good way to start beating it.

Then consider together three ways people can deal with worries:

1 **Naming the worry:** Take the 'Naming the Worry' slips you have prepared in advance (text below) and read out each slip in turn. Ask, 'What is this child worried about?', and get the children to name the worry. There are lots of right answers to each one so almost anything goes. The idea is that the children begin to notice that people get worried sometimes, but can do something about it. Suggest that the first step is to admit the worry: 'I feel worried about …'

## Text for 'Naming the Worry'

| |
|---|
| Pete feels sick when he stands on the high board at the pool. |
| Nadia does not want to go round to her nan's. |
| On a Sunday night Liam feels more worried than on a Thursday night. |
| Tracey sleeps with the light on. |
| Jai won't watch nature programmes on TV. |

What do the children think any of these people can do about their worries?

Now do a brainstorm of any other worries that children might have. Introduce the idea that having a name for your worry is the first step towards beating it. What do people think about this? As appropriate, children may be able to say aloud: 'I am sometimes worried about …'

2 **Sharing the worry:** Ask the children to make and decorate their own 'worry boxes', into which they will 'post' their worries. Younger children may need an adult to help, and small groups might like to work to create a common box or boxes. First make a slit in the side of the box, and then encourage the children to decorate their boxes in any way they like. You could suggest: an animal face 'eating up' the worries, a building to 'contain' them, or a representation of a real post box. Decide on a way to share the worry and work out what to do about it: could it be shared in 'circle time', during a one-to-one session with an adult, or in some other way?

3 **Worry Warrior (Action):** often DOING something is the best way to take control of worries, for example: telling someone how you feel; going to a place you feel safe; using a worry stone; trying out a little bit of the worrying thing with support (e.g. closing the door a tiny bit more each night if you are worried about the dark). Discuss this idea and ask what people do, or could do.

## Extensions

- What other ways can we deal with worries? Make a video of 'Top Tips' for other children.
- The child or group could write, tell and illustrate a story about a boy, girl, or animal who finds a way to deal with a worry. This could be bound into a big illustrated book.
- Try, ideally, to build 'being a worry warrior' into the children's schedule and routine, rather than using this activity as a one-off.



*Page 3 of 3*

# Activity 3
# Relaxation Tools

☑ Individuals ☑ Small groups ☑ Whole class

## Aims

This activity is about trying out some active ways to relax. These can be built into the school day or done at home. Ideally they are planned into a day-to-day programme, rather than being called on when you are feeling stressed!

## Materials

A quiet space (perhaps sitting or lying on a gym mat, in an armchair, or lying on a bed); good quality bubble-blowing bottles & wands.

## Activity

- Make sure you will not be disturbed.
- Ask the children to settle down in the chosen quiet space.
- No one should speak!
- Make sure everyone has their own space.
- Encourage children to close their eyes, although they do not have to.

Take some time in this first stage and put some calming music on whilst everyone settles themselves down in their spot. Use a countdown to make sure everyone gets settled in time. You can use each of the three tools in turn if you want, or choose to focus on only one in a session.

## Tool 1

Tell the children that they will be tensing (squeezing tightly) each big muscle in their body for about 5–10 seconds and then relaxing it. Make sure everyone knows how to do this by demonstrating first, for example: say 'squeeze', and then 'relax' whilst scrunching up and then relaxing your whole face.

Use the script that follows to get the children to tense and relax different muscles in turn, each time saying, 'Tense the muscles in [your arms] 3-2-1 [counting down to 1] … relax':

(a) your arms
(b) your hands
(c) your legs and feet
(d) your stomach
(e) your shoulders
(f) your neck
(g) your face

How did you find that? Did it help you relax?

## Tool 2: Counting relaxation

Dim the lights and use the following script:

> Close your eyes.
>
> Count slowly to 10 out loud.
>
> Slowly open your eyes.
>
> Close your eyes again.
>
> Now count slowly to 10 in your head.
>
> Slowly open your eyes
>
> How did you find that? Did it help you relax?

## Tool 3: Blowing bubbles

Explain that everyone is going to concentrate on their breathing today, because this can help people to relax.

> Close your eyes.
>
> Listen to your breathing. Think about your breathing.
>
> Breathe in slowly, breathe out slowly.
>
> Try to get a nice long breath out.

Model this clearly. It can be helpful to suggest children imagine that they are smelling a lovely flower as they breathe in; as they breathe out they are slowly blowing out a candle flame.

Now give out the bubble bottles and wands and let everyone have a go at blowing nice big bubbles (this part of the activity could take place outside and there is no need to stay calm and quiet!)

Back inside again, return to Tool 3, breathing slowly in and slowly out. Suggest that, as they are blowing out, they remember what it was like to be blowing bubbles and try to picture it in their heads.

# Activity 4
# Visualisation

## Aims

To practise visualisation as a way of feeling calm.

## Materials

A quiet space with no distractions; gym mats. Each person should have paper, coloured pencils or pens, paintbrushes and paper close by them in their quiet space.

## Activity

Lead the visualisation with the following script:

> Today we are going to visualise a peaceful place where we feel safe and calm.
>
> Start by closing your eyes and thinking about the kind of place that makes you feel calm.
>
> Next open your eyes and draw or paint your peaceful place.
>
> When you are finished, show [me]a friend your picture. Think and talk about the following:
>
> - What can you see?
> - What can you feel?
> - What can you hear?
> - What can you smell?
>
> Now close your eyes again and *imagine* your peaceful place. This means seeing and feeling it in your head – try to make a picture in your mind.
>
> You could use this image any time you want to feel calm. How could you do this? When would it work best?
>
> Try it again. Is it getting easier?

Activity Sheet 4

# Activity 5
# Face Your Fears

☑ **Individuals**

## Aims

This activity is about helping individual children to get over their fears by slow, supported exposure to those fears. It should only be done on a one-to-one basis with children who have an identified fear and who have some awareness and understanding that they have a fear.

## Materials

Worksheet 3 'Sample Fear Ladder' & Worksheet 4 'Facing My Fear', pencil.

## Activity

The idea is to slowly and gently introduce an anxiety-reducing strategy by supporting the child through steady exposure to the feared object or situation. The child learns to tolerate the feared object or situation by means of a series of very gentle steps, beginning with the least anxiety-producing aspect of the process and ending with the most difficult step. It should always follow the child's lead and is important to remember that it is counter-productive to push children.

### Step One

Identify exactly what the child is afraid of. Remember that fear is a natural response to situations perceived as threatening. Being afraid 'sometimes' does not always mean you need help. Before doing this activity be clear that the child would benefit from help – if the answer is 'yes' to these three questions then the child is likely to benefit from some structured help:

1. Is there an obvious source of their fear?
2. Is their fear interfering with their day-to-day functioning?
3. Do they show some sign that they want help to deal with their fear?

*Page 1 of 2*

Observe the child carefully over time and talk to those around them to help identify exactly what the feared object or situation is. Asking the child what they are afraid of is unlikely, on its own, to give a clear picture of what the feared object is.

## Step Two

Construct the 'Anxiety Hierarchy'. This involves working out as many gentle steps as possible to build up exposure to the feared thing. For example, if the child is afraid of dogs, a hierarchy may begin with hearing about a dog or looking at a picture of one. A brief example is given on Worksheet 3, 'Sample Fear Ladder'.

## Step Three

Work with the child to create their own fear ladder, using Worksheet 4, 'Facing My Fear'. Ask the child to write down all the gentle, easy steps they think they could take to face and conquer their fear. Then, begin at the easiest step on the ladder and build up very, very slowly, noticing and celebrating with the child every step of the way. The task is to build up good evidence over time that it is okay to be with the feared object – that fears are not there forever and that we can do something about them. It is important for the child to feel part of a team with their trusted adult when working up the ladder. Over the weeks that follow, schedule in regular time to work slowly together on conquering the fear, making sure to record progress with the worksheet.

# Worksheet 3
# Sample Fear Ladder

Use the fear ladder to overcome your fear slowly!

First look at the example below, about overcoming a fear of dogs.

Then use the blank worksheet that follows to find tactics for overcoming your own fear, step by step.

| Step | Date started | Date completed | Comments |
|---|---|---|---|
| Listen to a story about a dog. | | | |
| Be in the same room as a picture of a dog. | | | |
| Hold a picture of a dog. | | | |
| Watch a 10-second video of a dog when with an adult I trust. | | | |
| Watch (with an adult I trust) a 20-second video of a dog playing with a child. | | | |
| Watch the same 20-second video of a dog playing with a child, with an adult I trust. | | | |
| Be in the same building as a dog. | | | |
| Can you think of more easy steps? | | | |

# Worksheet 4

## Facing My Fear

| Step | Date started | Date completed | Comments |
|---|---|---|---|
| | | | |
| | | | |
| | | | |
| | | | |
| | | | |
| | | | |
| | | | |
| | | | |
| | | | |
| | | | |

Worksheet 4

# Activity 6
# Anger Antics

## Aims

This activity is about noticing and naming anger so as to start regulating it. We do not want children to stop feeling angry! But it can be helpful to control strong emotions like anger sometimes and learn to manage them. This activity could be used with a child who seems to need help managing anger. It is best done one-to-one.

## Materials

Picture cards on Worksheet 5, 'Anger Picture Cards': enlarge on a photocopier, laminate and cut the cards up. Large piece of paper (big enough for the child to lie down on), crayons, coloured pencils or felt-tip pens.

## Activity

Anger is usually a normal and helpful response. However, it can be overwhelming and difficult. It can be a secondary emotion, for example: a response to feeling anxious, or scared, or frustrated, rather than being the first thing we feel.

Young children are likely to have little awareness of emotion regulation, which is developmentally normal.

The first step is to help children understand what anger is – to put a name to it and to begin to recognise it as a feeling, including what happens in their bodies when they feel it. There are many individual differences.

Ask the child to pick one of the picture cards (Worksheet 5) that they think shows their anger. Ask them to give their anger a name (e.g., volcano). Discuss why they picked that card and that name. The child should lead here, rather than the adult suggesting names or explanations. If none of the cards is right for them they can draw their own image or make a model.

*Page 1 of 2*

The next step is to think with the child about what is happening in their bodies when anger (or whatever name they have picked) comes along. Get the child to lie on a big piece of paper and draw around the outline. Draw and colour on the outline to show what is happening when anger comes along. The more detail the better.

Practise an 'anger sentence' with the child that they could use when they notice the warning signs in their bodies, for example: 'I feel angry'; 'Volcano is going to blow/erupt'; 'I can feel IT'.

An extension to this activity could be to start making up, writing down, or telling some personal anger stories. The anger character they have named could be the star of the tale(s). Work with the child to think of things that can be done to control and calm this character – what have they noticed?

# Worksheet 5

## Anger Picture Cards

Worksheet 5

# Activity 7
# Thought Bubbles

## Aims

This activity should not be done with children who have very little language, poor attention, or poor self-awareness compared to their peers. The purpose of the activity is to notice thoughts. Ideally this extends to building awareness that we have some control over our thoughts, for example: having positive thoughts can help us feel better and behave differently.

## Materials

Worksheet 6 'Thought Bubbles' & Worksheet 7 'Challenging NATs': laminate Worksheet 6 or stick to card and cut the sections out individually so that the blank thought bubble and three thought bubble scenarios may be used separately.

## Activity

Start the session with a discussion: What is a thought?

Use the empty thought bubble from Worksheet 6. If working with one child, take it in turns to hold the bubble over each other's heads and guess each other's thoughts. In a small group, each child takes a turn to do this, going all members of the group.

Apply the same thought-guessing activity with each character in the three different scenarios on Worksheet 6.

## Extension

The extension asks children to reframe Negative Automatic Thoughts (NATs). This exercise is only for older children with good language skills, attention skills, self-awareness and grasp of the theory of mind (awareness that other people have thoughts different to our own).

Explain that we should challenge our negative thoughts and always check out the evidence! Use the grid on Worksheet 7 and work with the child or group to think about how we could change negative thoughts into more balanced thoughts (the first one is done for you).

# Worksheet 6
# Thought Bubbles

Worksheet 6

*Page 1 of 2*

# Worksheet 6
## Thought Bubbles

Scenario 2

Scenario 3

Page 2 of 2

# Worksheet 7

# Automatic Negative Thoughts (NATs)

| NAT | REFRAME IT! |
|---|---|
| I can't do that! | It is difficult, but I can ask for help. |
| I always get left out at play time! | |
| My work is the worst! | |
| It is always my fault! | |
| He thinks I'm rubbish! | |

Worksheet 7

# Activity 8
# I Can't Do It … Yet!

☑ **Individuals** 

## Aims

This activity is about cultivating a 'growth mindset' and introduces the idea that perseverance and hopefulness are qualities worth 'growing' in ourselves.

## Materials

Before the session, decide on the tasks that the child or children will be asked to complete and make available any necessary props (e.g., using the examples below: marbles & track; sand tray & tools; tracing paper, pencils & items to trace; bowl of water & a jug); photographs of the child or children at different stages in their life. Optional: other visual aids that emphasise the idea of 'growing skills' as we get older, for example: three flowerpots & cut-out magazine pictures of young children doing things at different stages, early in their lives.

## Activity

The activity should introduce and reinforce the following ideas: just because you can't do it now, does not mean you never will be able to do it; other people can help you improve at things; practice helps.

Set up a range of activities, some of which the children can do easily, some of which they cannot do easily. Include some activities that the child cannot yet do. Allow free play.

Examples of activities to try:

- Marble run
- Sandcastle building
- Tracing
- Pouring water

*Page 1 of 2*

After a period of free play in which the adult is observing, give some targeted mediation. Mediate to help and guide the child, but give just the right amount of help. Some degree of challenge should remain, but the task should be achievable with the support of the adult.

Examples of mediation strategies:

1 Encouraging perseverance, frustration tolerance and attention skills

2 Encouraging flexible thinking and suggesting different approaches

3 Breaking down the task into steps

4 Reminding and praising.

Use the following script often:

To reinforce the point that we get better at things when we keep doing them and keep on trying, get some pictures of the child or group members as a baby, as a 3-year-old, and as a 5-year-old (assuming you are working with 5-year-olds). Think with them of examples of things they could do at each stage. This can be presented visually, for example: three flower pots with photographs of a child at three different ages stuck to them. Age-appropriate skills can be shown 'growing' from the pots, using pictures of children doing things, from crawling, standing up, to building something complex like a Lego tower or a sandcastle.

It is a good idea to join up with home on this task if doing it at nursery.

# Activity 9
# A Good Mistake

☑ **Individuals** 

## Aims

Sometimes we forget that mistakes can be positive. Henry Ford said that the only bad mistake is the one we do not learn from.

## Materials

Paper, coloured pencils or crayons.

## Activity

Read the following story about a good mistake:

### A Good Mistake

Percy the cat was very good at cleaning his ears. He was sure that he had the cleanest ears of all the cats in Castle Gardens.

He was not sure anyone had noticed, but he was proud anyway. Sometimes he admired himself in the pool in the middle of the gardens.

One day Percy was admiring his ears when Meowford, the cat from next door, came up behind him and meowed quietly: 'What dirty ears! Do you want me to teach you how to clean them?'

Percy was shocked and upset.

'I have lovely clean ears, thank you very much,' he meowed grumpily back.

*Page 1 of 2*

'Not from the back you don't. I can show you how to clean them if you like,' said Meowford.

Percy had never thought about cleaning the back of his ears before. What an idea!

He was just about to tell Meowford to mouse off, when he changed his mind.

I can learn from this, he thought.

'Yes please do show me,' Percy said to Meowford, thinking to himself: I can make a new friend and get even cleaner ears at the same time!

Ask the children what they thought of the story and lead a discussion of these questions:

- What does 'mistake' mean?
- Why is the story called 'A Good Mistake'?
- Can mistakes ever be good?
- Did Percy do the right thing?
- Why, or why not?
- Why did Percy choose to let Meowford help him?
- Have you ever made a 'good mistake'?

As appropriate, introduce the idea that if we make mistakes we can learn.

Do some illustrations for the story – read it again, if necessary.

## Extension

Make up your own story called 'A Good Mistake'.

# Activity 10
# My Feelings

## Aims

Learning to explore emotions and use the vocabulary of feelings.

## Materials

Worksheet 8 'Feelings Faces' & Worksheet 9 'Emotion Cards': laminate the worksheets, then cut them up into individual cards.

## Activity

Start by helping the child to understand what a feeling is. Until they have some idea about this, Activity 10 should not be attempted! Some ways to do this are:

1 **Modelling.** The adult names the feeling and acts it out.

2 **Stories.** Read a favourite tale with a focus on how the characters feel – name those feelings and act them out.

3 **Sentence stems and repetition.** For example, 'I feel angry, because he hit me'; 'I feel sad, because she took my toy'; 'I feel excited, because we are going to the zoo'; 'I feel angry, because …'; 'I feel sad, because …'; 'I feel excited, because …'

Now use the cards on the worksheets to name some feelings together. These cards can be used in many different situations. They can be used as an activity to discuss feelings, at transitions during the day, or before going on to other activities, such as Activity 2, 'Worry Warrior', or Activity 5, 'Face Your Fears'.

You may use the 'Feelings Faces' and 'Emotion Cards' together or separately. With both sets, children will focus on the pictures and be encouraged to use their own words for feelings – do not worry if their word does not match the one on the card! Adults can model and name their own feelings and those on the cards to help children develop their emotional vocabulary.

*Page 1 of 2*

Some suggestions for using the cards:

- Ask the child to pick two cards that they like – why these two?
- Ask the child to pick a card they do not understand – discuss.
- Pick five cards randomly and discuss.
- Ask the child to put the cards in groups.
- Ask the child to use the cards to tell a story.
- Pick a card and say to the child, 'This is how I feel today – how do you feel?
- Use the cards as part of a game, for example: 'Snap' (when you get a snap, name the feeling); or 'Pairs' (place the cards face down on a surface, each player turning two cards over per go. The aim is to match two cards. When the match is achieved, the feeling matched should be named). Children could also make up their own games.
- Set up a 'hunt the feeling' game, with cards hidden around the room or building or playground. At the end children can show their cards and name each feeling.

# Worksheet 8

# Feelings Faces

| | | |
|---|---|---|
| angry | unhappy | jealous |
| frustrated | sad | scared |
| excited | stressed | confused |
| cross | suspicious | nervous |
| happy | anxious | relaxed |

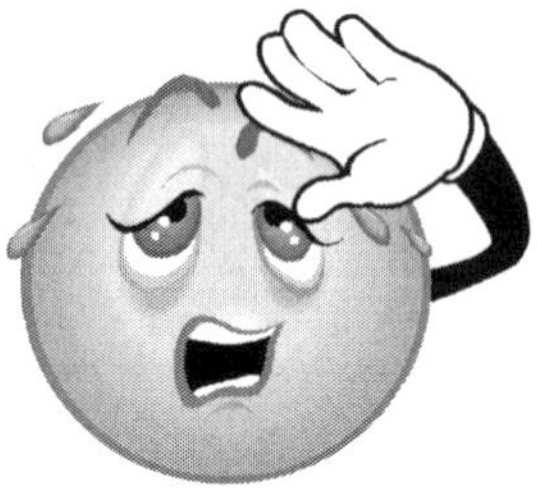

Worksheet 8

# Worksheet 9
# Emotion Cards

Confused

Lonely

Excited

Looked after

Cross

Bored

Page 1 of 3

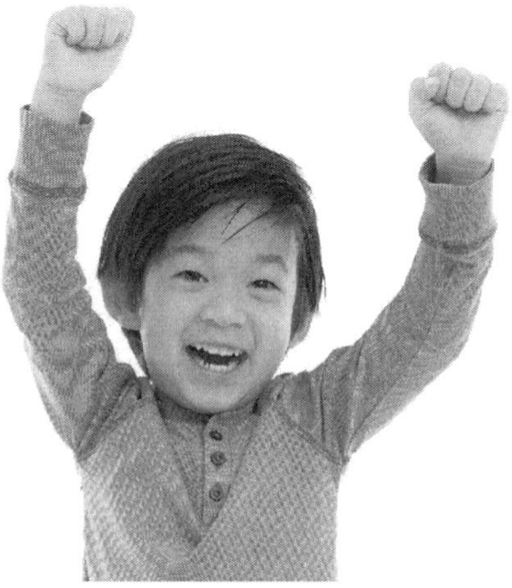

Happy

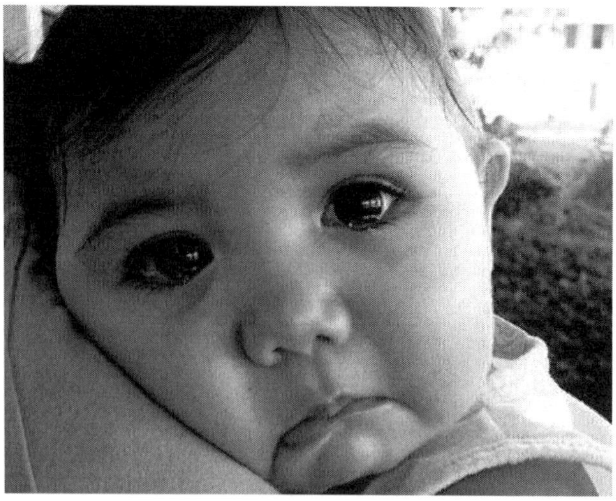

Sad

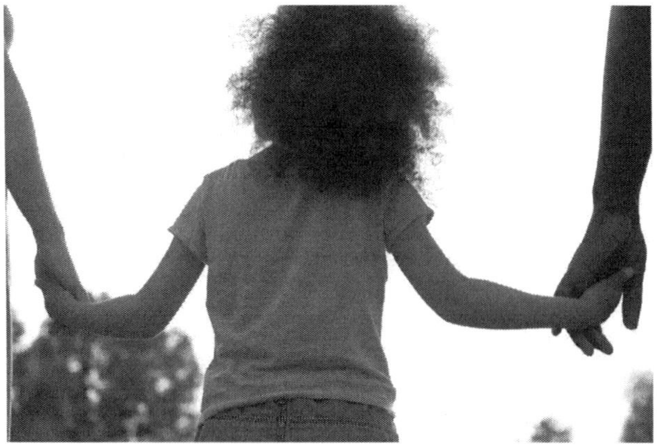

Safe

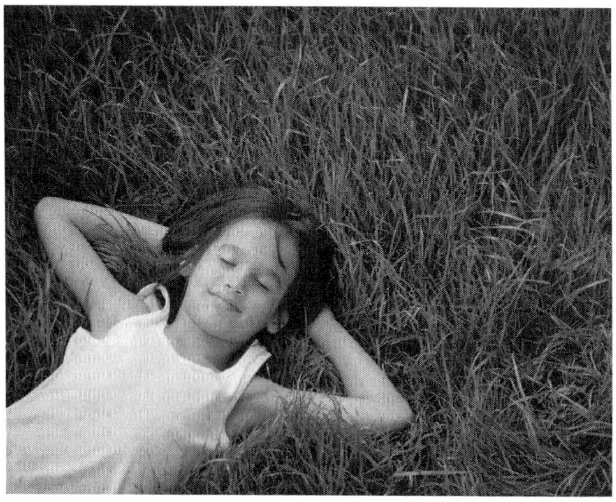

Relaxed

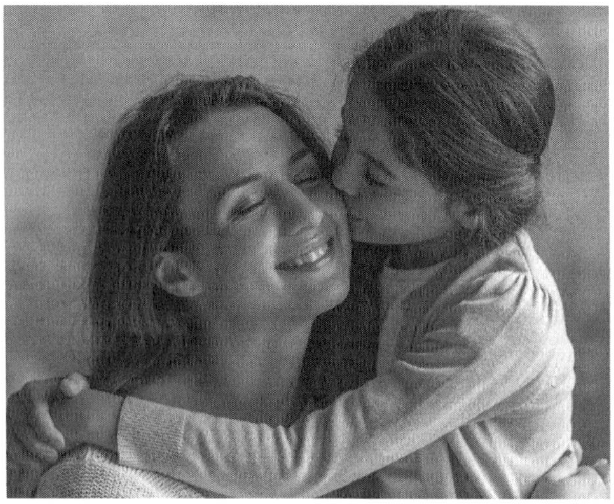

Loved

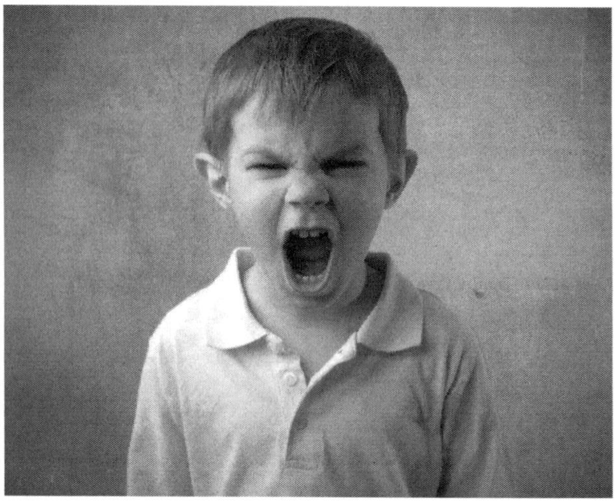

Angry

*Page 2 of 3*

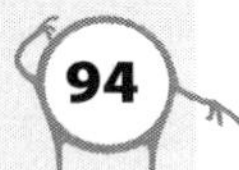

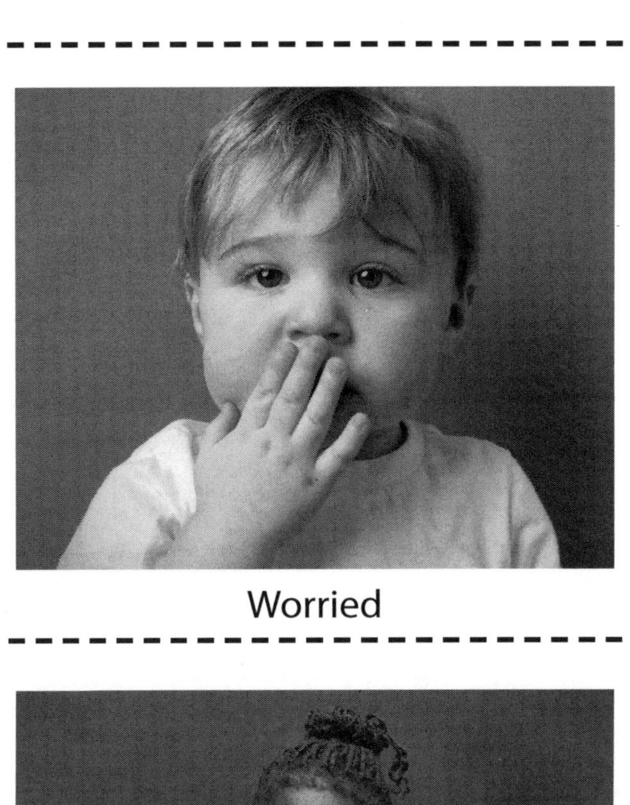
Worried

Scared

Proud

Independent

Strong

Afraid

Worksheet 9

Page 3 of 3

# Activity 11

# My Day

 **Individuals**  **Small groups**  **Whole class**

## Aims

In this journaling activity, the idea is to notice how we feel and to take time to notice good things that happen each day – it is a positive record or diary.

## Materials

Scrapbook for each child; collage materials, box of pictures cut from magazines, emoji stickers or print-outs (you could use the 'Feelings Faces' cards from Activity 10); pens and pencils, glue; photocopies of Worksheet 10, 'My Day', if needed.

## Activity

This is a journaling activity for the early years. Children make a scrapbook to record their feelings and experiences each day: encourage them to decorate and illustrate their books, look back over them, and share them with others.

Scrapbooks need not be completed every day. They could be done once a week or every day for a weekly block (for example).

### Suggested sections

1 At the front children could construct an 'All about Me' page with illustrations of things they like and important information about them, for example: photographs of family and friends, pets, favourite food, colour, game, when I grow up …, and so on.

2 Each scrapbook entry should include a record of 'My Feelings Today'. This can be done by picking a card or sticker and gluing it in, by drawing a picture, by selecting an emoji, by using a word that an adult writes in, by choosing a picture from a selection. Children may put in as many or as few feelings as they would like. They may also be able to add what made them feel that way.

*Page 1 of 2*

3. Each scrapbook entry should include a record of: 'Good things that happened today'. This can be in the form of words, pictures, cartoons, collage, cut and stick.
4. Each scrapbook entry should include a record of: 'People I enjoyed being with today'. Children may like to stick in photographs, say names aloud to be written down by the adult, or draw.
5. Any other sections that the child would like (as long as they are positive!) can be added also.

An example of layout is included on Worksheet 10 (and may be photocopied for children to use, if necessary), but there are many ways to do this, for example: by creating a video diary, collaging, audio recording, card box, or drawing.

# Worksheet 10

## My Day

Day: ______________________________

My Feelings Today

Page 1 of 2

Good Things that Happened Today
People Today

# Activity 12
# The Problem-Solving Tree & Flower

☑ Individuals  

☑ Individuals ☑ Small groups ☑ Whole class

## Aims

Supporting the acquisition of problem-solving skills.

## Materials

Worksheet 11, 'The Ant & the Bee Flashcards'; laminate and cut out into individual cards; very large sheets of paper, coloured pens or felt-tips. Optional: camera & labels, if using an image of a real tree; coloured tissue paper & pipe cleaners to make the flower.

## Activity

This activity is about problem-solving. Introduce the topic by telling the children that they will be thinking about problems and how to solve them.

The focus will be a story stem: start by reading the 'The Ant and the Bee'. You can use the flashcards on Worksheet 11 to help you tell the story.

> The ant and the bee lived on Kitjay Street. Both of them were lonely, because they lived on their own. Ants and bees do not like living on their own. Neither the ant nor the bee spoke to anyone else on the street. Ever.
>
> One day the ant was collecting a grain of sugar from the garden when he fell in a hole. He tripped over a piece of leaf he had left out the day before and fell right in. He tried and tried, but could not get out.
>
> At the same time the bee was flying up and down Kitjay Street, feeling bored and lonely ...

Now work through one or both of these thinking tools to come up with some ideas to help the ant. We will be problem-solving detectives.

## Thinking tool 1: Problem-solving tree

- Draw a big tree on a big piece of paper up on the wall or in the middle of the floor. You could even add labels to a real tree and take photographs.

- On the trunk show the problem (e.g., the ant fell in a hole; the bee is lonely) by writing, drawing or using one or more flashcards.
- If the children are developmentally ready, on the roots show what caused the problem (e.g., the hole, the ant, the bee, bad luck) by writing, drawing or using one or more flashcards.
- On the branches show some ideas to solve the problem (e.g., the bee flies to the rescue) by writing, drawing or making a new flashcard.
- If the children are developmentally ready, on the leaves show what might happen if you use that solution (e.g., the ant and the bee become friends) by writing, drawing or making a new flashcard.

*Page 2 of 3*

## Thinking tool 2: Problem-solving flower

- Draw a big flower on a big piece of paper up on the wall or on the floor. You could also make a collage of a big flower, using tissue paper and pipe cleaners.

- On the stem show the problem.
- On each petal show one thing that could be done to solve the problem.
- In the centre of the flower write the chosen solution.

# Worksheet 11

# The Ant & the Bee Flashcards

| | |
|---|---|
|  Ant |  Bee |
|   Lonely |  Hole in the garden |
|  Kitjay street |  Grain of Sugar |

# Activity 13
# Goals Rocket & Overcoming Your Gremlins

☑ **Individuals**  **Small groups**  **Whole class**

## Aims

Supporting a child to overcome worry and plan for personal goals.

## Materials

Worksheet 12 'My Goals Rocket' & Worksheet 13 'My Gremlins'; pencils or pens.

Activity Sheet 13

## Activity

Use the worksheets to think about goals the child wants to reach ('My Goals Rocket') and things they may have to overcome on the way ('My Gremlins'). This is useful for children who are finding it difficult to do something due to worry or anxiety. It can also be useful in supporting children to think about something they want to work towards.

The worksheets should be filled in with an adult during a one-to-one session. In the first session, when the child is setting their goal and thinking about the difficulties they may have on the way ('My Goals Rocket'), the two of you should also think about who might help them reach their goal, or encouraging things that might help them, for example: 'My friends will cheer me on.' Then consider what rewards they would enjoy as they complete each step in achieving the goal. There is space on the worksheet for this support and those rewards to be recorded.

*Page 1 of 2*

Goals work best when they are child-led.

**Example of a goal:** To climb to the top of a climbing frame.

Example of how this goal might be broken down:

1 Visit climbing frame with my teacher.
2 Watch Robert climb the climbing frame.
3 Climb half way up with Robert.
4 Climb half way up on my own.
5 Climb all the way up on my own.

Then move on to the next worksheet and decide on the obstacles to reaching the goal – 'My Gremlins'. Gremlins are best identified in a session using open-ended questions. When filling in Worksheet 13, make sure the child understands what a gremlin is!

After the initial session, each step identified on Worksheet 12 may have to be practised a few times before moving on to the next. 'My Goals Rocket' should be referred to regularly, with appropriate rewards and praise for achievement! 'My Goals Rocket' could be laminated and put up on the wall.

# Worksheet 12
# My Goals Rocket

Name: ____________________________________________

| Help I need | Rewards |
|---|---|
| ____________________ | ____________________ |
| ____________________ | ____________________ |
| ____________________ | ____________________ |

*Chart 1: My Goals Rocket*

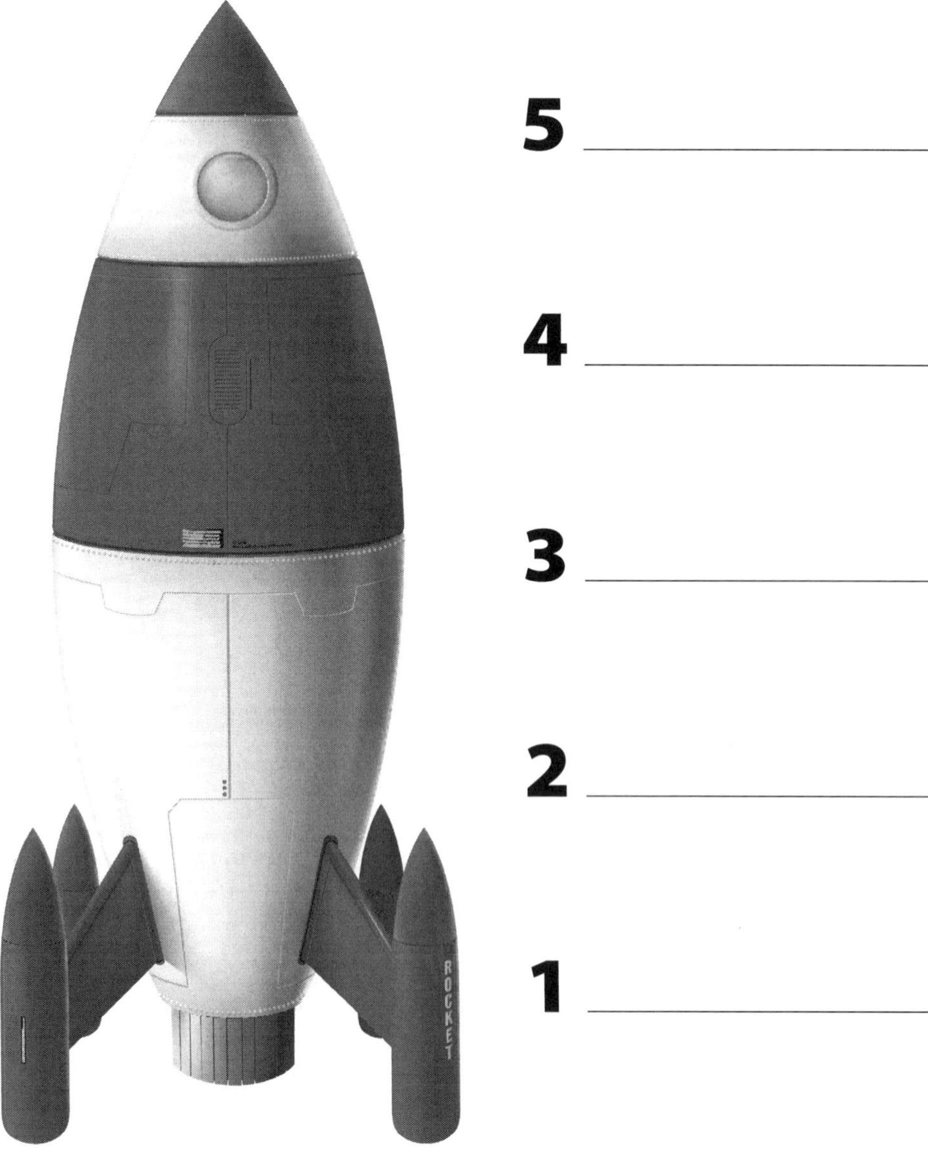


5 ______________________________

4 ______________________________

3 ______________________________

2 ______________________________

1 ______________________________

# Worksheet 13
# My Gremlins

*Chart 2: My Gremlins*

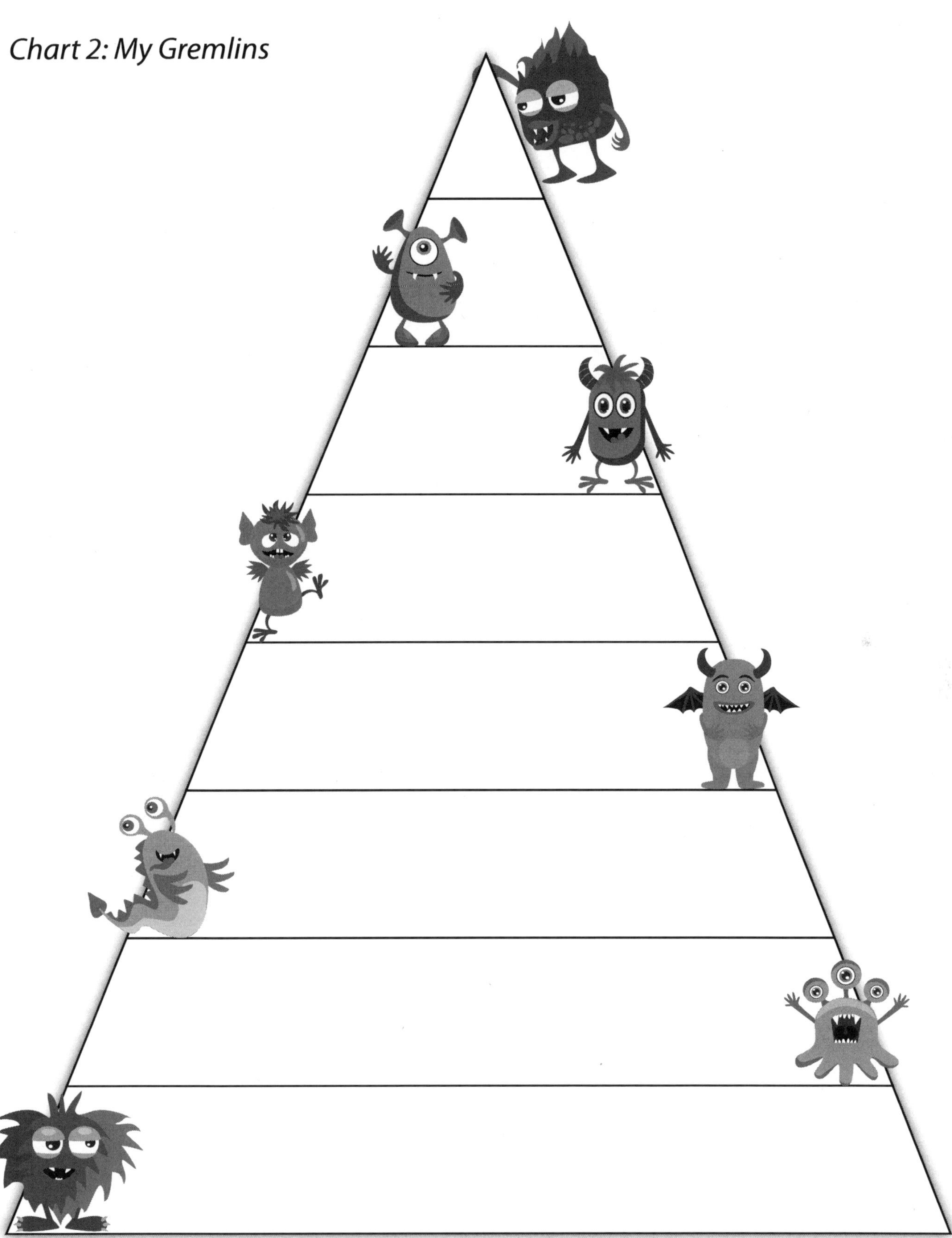

# Activity 14
# My Mountain

## Aims

Encouraging children to identify their personal goals and to persevere in working towards them.

## Materials

Worksheet 14, 'Mountain & Achievement Flashcards', Blutack®; enlarge and laminate or stick to card and cut out the set of Achievement Flashcards.

## Activity

In this activity the children take time to notice the things they can do on their own; the things they can do with help, and the things they want to do, but cannot do yet.

Put the three mountain cards up around the room: 'I Can ...'; 'I Can with Help'; 'I Want to ...'.

First, model the activity. Take an Achievement Card from the box and name the activity. Then stick it up next to one of the mountains, for example: 'I Can ... ride a bike with help'; 'I Can ... draw'; I Want to ... climb a wall'.

Help the children to do the same until you have lots of photographs up around the room showing achievements and aspirations. Add more pictures as needed.

Celebrate your successes!

# Worksheet 14
# Mountain & Achievement Flashcards

Mountain 1:
'I Can'

Mountain 2:
'I Can with Help'

Mountain 3:
'I Want to'

# Activity 15
# Mood Marbles

## Aims

A method for reflecting on and recording feelings.

## Materials

Marbles in a variety of sizes & colours; a glass jar each; sticky labels or photographs of the children to personalise their jars; Worksheet 15, 'Mood Marbles Tracker', for each person.

## Activity

Each child labels their own 'mood jar'. Encourage them to track their emotions by filling a jar with 'mood marbles': each day they can pick a marble that they feel expresses their mood that day.

As they add their daily marble, they may like to note the significant events of the day and their feelings using Worksheet 15, for example: 'fell over and felt sad'; 'got a sticker and felt proud'; or, 'had fun playing and felt happy'. This activity may be completed daily before going home, or immediately after a specific activity. Alternatively, the facilitator may also choose to complete the 'Mood Marbles Tracker' themselves, and share it with the child, as appropriate.

There are no right answers here and children should be encouraged to pick marbles independently. Model the phrase: 'I felt …'

Try to focus on positive feelings, at least at first.

This activity can also be used to rate the mood before an event or activity, and again afterwards to track how they felt during the event. Give the children time to discuss their feelings.

# Worksheet 15
# Mood Marbles Tracker

| Date | Marbles Chosen | Why | Mood |
|---|---|---|---|
| | | | |
| | | | |
| | | | |
| | | | |
| | | | |
| | | | |
| | | | |
| | | | |

# Activity 16
# Stop & Think About the Good Times!

## Aims

Stopping and reflecting on positive events; increasing awareness of thought processes.

## Materials

Child-proof/child-friendly camera or tablet (one each); computer/printer access to collect and print the pictures. Optional: scrapbook, glue, pens/pencils to record experiences.

## Activity

Wouldn't life be great if you could make good things happen more often and make bad things happen less often? This simple idea is the basis of a powerful tool used by people in many different walks of life: stopping and thinking about good or bad experiences and working out how to repeat the good ones, while avoiding the bad ones. The process can be broken down into four steps, listed below

### 1 Experience

You focus on something that happened that was really good or really bad.

### 2 Feelings

You find the words for how you felt about it. Get everything off your chest, so that later you can think more clearly.

Page 1 of 2

## 3 Thinking

You figure out, calmly and rationally, what you can do to avoid the bad experiences and repeat the good ones.

## 4 Action

You plan what to do next time.

Young children are not developmentally ready to use a framework like this and should not be pushed to do so. However, they can notice what they like and what they do not like. This activity is about noticing the good times.

The task is to give the children a camera each for an hour or so (over a number of days if possible) and let them take photographs of whatever they like. Model this idea first by using a camera yourself and taking some photographs of things you like (e.g., an apple, your friend, the sand tray). Whilst taking the photographs, say aloud, for example: 'I love apples'; 'playing with Sajid makes me feel happy.'

This works best if you give a clear demonstration and then trust the child to have a go. We are interested in what they like and should try not to guide and structure them too much.

Once you have a good collection of pictures, print them off and sort through them with the child, always reinforcing the idea that these are pictures of what they like and enjoy and what makes them feel good. When sorting, try to pick up on which the child likes best and put others to one side. This editing can also be done on a computer.

By the end of the process you should hopefully have a selection of photographs that show 'Good Times' for the child. These can be displayed or made into a book.

## Extension

It the child seems able to notice their feelings and has some emotional vocabulary, you might ask, 'How do you feel?', or use the sentence stem, 'I feel …', while looking at the photographs. You can model this language with your own selection of photographs. The 'Feelings Faces' cards used in Activity 10 may be helpful here (Worksheet 8).

*Page 2 of 2*

# Activity 17
# Magic Circles

☑ Individuals ☑ Small groups ☑ Whole class

## Aims

Supports a change in focus to positive, rather than negative, events.

## Materials

Pictures/video clips of enjoyable things to stimulate reflection. A very large piece of paper for each child (e.g., two pieces of sugar paper, taped together); crayons or felt-tip pens; a photograph of each child; collage materials (fabric, string, glue, wool, etc.); copies of Worksheet 16, 'Magic Circles'. Optional: magazine pictures showing active people experiencing positive emotions.

## Activity

In this activity we are thinking about something we have really enjoyed. Start by telling the children this and by giving the children some examples of things *you* have really enjoyed, including pictures or video clips. It is important to provide visuals rather than just use words. Name them simply and clearly, and name your feelings simply and clearly, for example: 'I enjoyed trampolining. I felt excited.'

Now lay out the large pieces of paper on the floor, one for each child, and draw around the children's outlines. In a large group, children could work in pairs to trace their partner's outline. Each person adds a photograph of their face to the outline and some collage materials, as appropriate and if time allows.

*Page 1 of 2*

Now each person draws three circles on their sheet:

- Circle 1 (around the whole body) labelled: 'I did …' Encourage the children to give the activity, the people there, the place.
- Circle 2 (around or next to the stomach), labelled: 'I felt …' The 'Feelings Faces' cards from Activity 10 may be used, or just a selection of happy faces, such as those on Worksheet 15.
- Circle 3 (around or next to the head) labelled, 'I thought …' This could be as simple as writing 'hooray!'.

See Worksheet 16 for an example. Now start to fill the circles with pictures and/or words. Start with Circle 1.

Younger children or those developmentally unready to reflect on feelings and thoughts will just fill in the label for Circle 1. Some children may be able to fill in Circle 2 as well. Older children may be able to fill in Circle 3. It is important not to push children to fill in the labels for which they are not ready. It is fine to simply have a list in Circle 1 of lots of things they have done that they have liked. Follow the lead of the child.

A colour code can be used to match up experiences and emotions across the three circles, for example: a picture outlined in blue on the Circle 1 label: a smiley face outlined in blue for Circle 2; a speech bubble in blue for Circle 3.

# Worksheet 16
# Magic Circles

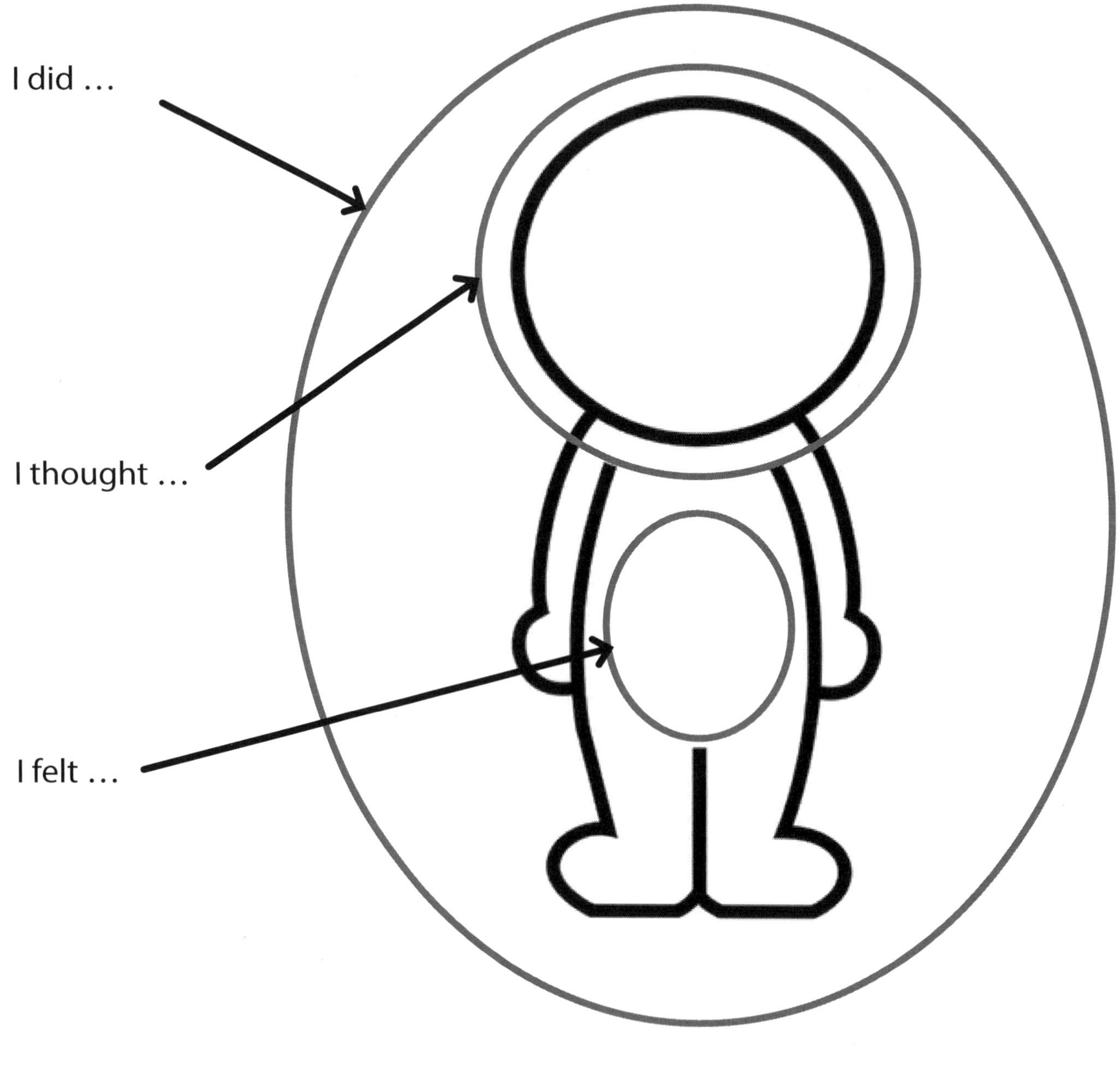

I did …

I thought …

I felt …

# Activity 18
# Oops!

☑ **Individuals**

## Aims

For children struggling to maintain a positive outlook, this activity focuses on seeing the positive in something that went 'wrong'. The idea is to identify the negative feeling or response and to be able to make the links between the thoughts and feelings whilst identifying the ways in which they can transform the initial negative thought.

## Materials

A very large piece of paper (e.g., two pieces of sugar paper, taped together); crayons or felt-tip pens; a photograph of the child; collage materials (fabric, string, glue, wool, etc.); a copy of Worksheet 17, 'Oops!'.

## Activity

This activity should only be used with children who seem to struggle to stay positive. If a child is not having this kind of issue do not use this activity, use only Activity 17. If you are doing Activity 18, do Activity 17 first.

This activity repeats Activity 17, but the focus is on noticing that if you think positively about something that is negative (substitute a positive thought for a negative reaction) it can have an effect on how you feel and what you do. Young children or those developmentally unready will not be able to make this connection and should simply be supported to notice when things go well (Activity 17).

However, older children may be able to complete the activity, reflecting on a situation that they did not like, for example: when they cried because another child took their toy. Try to communicate the idea that it is okay to get upset … but helpful to notice it.

*Page 1 of 2*

We would like children to develop language to say how they feel. An important part of this learning is through watching others, particularly adults. As with Activity 17, the adult should use an experience that involved a negative reaction to model the process first, for example: 'Mrs Whitaker took my pen' (Circle 1); 'I felt upset' (Circle 2); 'Mrs Whitaker doesn't like me, I will never speak to her again' (Circle 3; an unhelpful and 'wrong' thought).

The most important element in this activity is the next stage, or Circle 4: encouraging the child to 'transform' the negative reaction/thought in Circle 3 into a more positive thought (Circle 4). As children get older they can be supported to understand that if you think different things you get different results, for example: 'What if I thought, "Maybe Mrs Whitaker took it by accident, I could ask for it back."' Offer the child plenty of support in this process: your own modelling of a negative reaction transformed to a positive thought is crucial.

# Worksheet 17

## Oops!

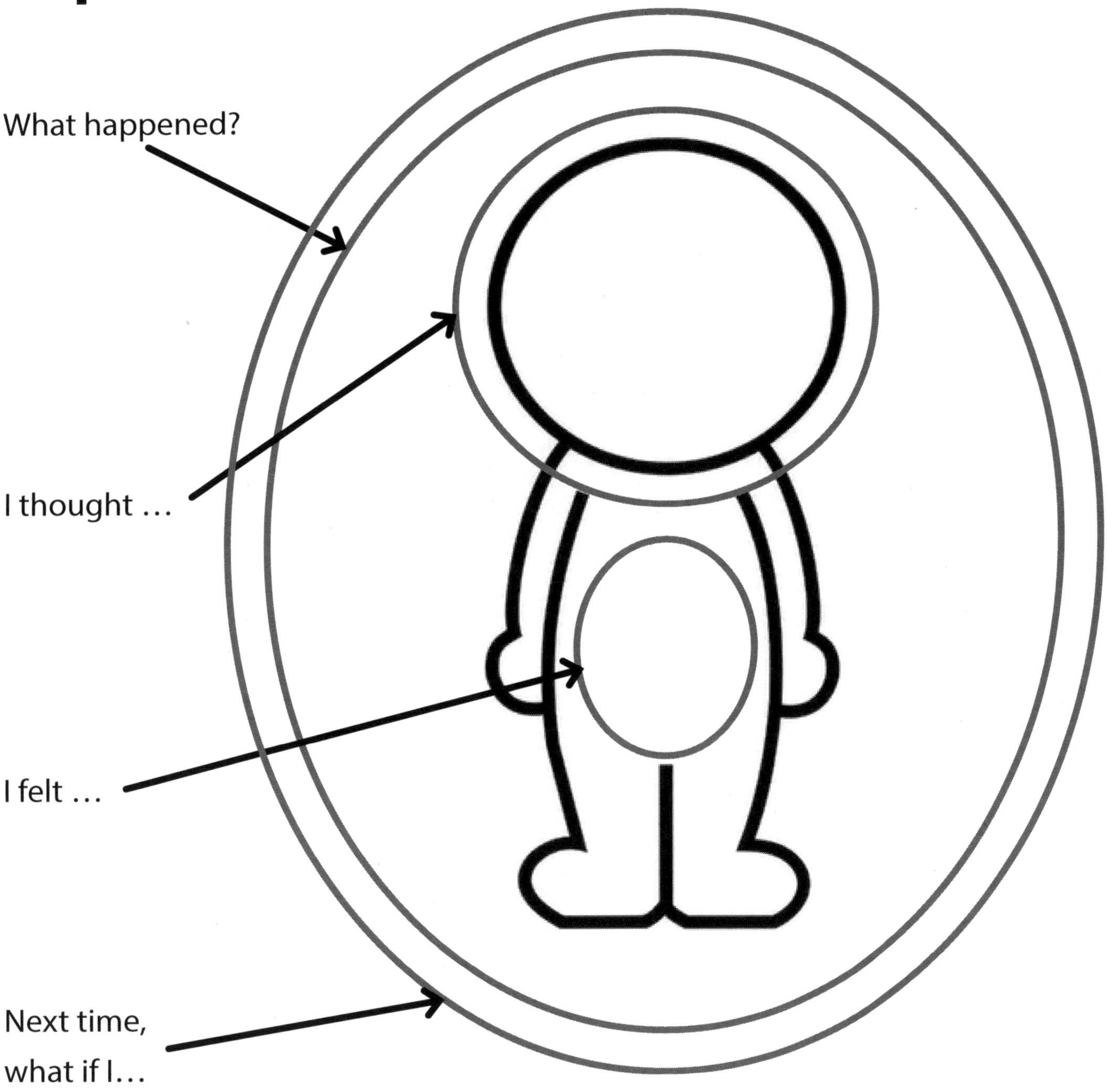

What happened?

I thought ...

I felt ...

Next time, what if I...

# Activity 19
# Magic Language

## Aims

To begin learning assertive, positive and appropriate language.

## Materials

Worksheet 18, 'Magic Language Script' (one each); pencils/pens.

## Activity

This activity is about communication. Sometimes people (of all ages) find it hard to say what they feel and what they want. In the early years children are learning to do this, but tend to use behaviour to tell us how they feel and what they want. In time we would like them to be able to use assertive language (saying what you feel and what you want without upsetting anyone or compromising your own needs).

To help them extend their use of assertive language, adults can consciously 'model' it: in other words, use it themselves. Children in the early years are unlikely to be ready to use this language themselves and should not be pushed to do so. We are simply modelling it as adults.

So, what do you model/say? Here are some simple rules for using 'magic language'.

- Use 'I' statements to say how you feel.
- Use an 'I' statement to say what you want.
- Try not to use 'You' statements, because people may think you are blaming them.

Page 1 of 2

## Modelling 'magic language'

When modelling 'magic language', you should:

- Speak clearly and simply in a short sentence.
- Repeat what you say.
- Use facial expression and other non-verbal communication to match what you are saying.
- Make sure that you are being genuine. This works best when you are expressing how you actually feel and what you actually want rather than play-acting!
- Model some positive self-talk and calming strategies, for example, instruct yourself (out loud) to 'breathe'.

Older children can be supported in starting to use 'magic language' themselves, but this should not be done until they are developmentally ready. Scripts such as the one on Worksheet 18 can be modelled by you and tried out by the children if their language and attention skills are good enough.

## Extension

Older (beyond the early years) children can practise saying a script to a video camera and watch themselves afterwards.

# Worksheet 18
# Magic Language Script

I feel ______________________________________________,

[angry, annoyed, furious, niggled, etc]

when ______________________________________________,

happens [say what happened]

because ______________________________________________.

[why it upsets you]

I would like ______________________________________________.

[what you want to happen or change]

You can ...

Learn this by heart!

# Activity 20
# What Lit the Fuse?

 Individuals  Very small groups

## Aims

To support children struggling with excessive anger.

## Materials

Internet access; large pieces of paper, coloured pens or pencils, paints, paint brushes, collage materials.

## Activity

This activity is for children who seem to struggle to control their anger. Those who feel angry (which is normal and useful!), but who regulate it well (for their age) should not do this task. The activity introduces the idea that anger has its 'triggers', which are different for different people. Most children will simply be thinking about what anger is like and that it usually happens as a result of something going on around them.

Start with a big piece of paper and write, 'I am angry', in the middle. Say it clearly: 'I am *angry*'. Act out being angry. Come obviously out of role. Look at some YouTube clips of people getting angry. Discuss as appropriate.

Sit quietly (ideally with eyes shut) and ask the child to think about what anger is like for them. Make sure that the child knows that it is normal to feel anger and that everyone experiences it differently. Sometimes it can make us feel bad. They should think about what anger is like *for them.*



*Page 1 of 2*

Now the children should create something that represents their anger, using drawing, painting, or collage, on the large piece of paper: they should get as many ideas down as possible. For example: What colour is the anger?; What is it like?; When does it come?; When does it not come?; Where does it turn up most?; Does it have a name?; Who is around when it comes?

Summarise simply by highlighting the things that seem to make anger come along – the *triggers*.

End by take a fresh piece of paper to display ideas (however crazy) about what we can do to take control of and manage our anger.

## Extension

You could extend this activity to start identifying personal triggers with older children and those with good language and some reflective ability.

# Activity 21
# My Good Deeds Ladder

## Aims

To focus on the positive in ourselves.

## Materials

Worksheet 19, 'My Good Deeds Ladder', pens/pencils.

## Activity

This activity is simply a record of good deeds the child has done. Try to add something each day, even if it is small. Ideally the child is involved in flagging up good deeds, but not all children will be able to do this and adults will need to notice, name and record good deeds. The record should be simple, visual and clear, for example, a sticker or picture stuck onto the ladder: Worksheet 19 may be used as a template. Rewards can be given on reaching different points on the ladder.

In this task the term 'good deeds' means good emotional literacy. Here are some examples of key emotional literacy skills to look out for:

- Listening
- Sharing
- Helping
- Being friendly
- Taking turns
- Thinking about how other people feel
- Noticing how we feel
- Being kind

# Worksheet 19

# My Good Deeds Ladder

Worksheet 19

# Activity 22
# Mindful Moments

## Aims

To learn relaxation techniques.

## Materials

Four cards giving the short steps in the four different Mindfulness techniques below; a box to hold the cards; bite-sized pieces of fruit in a bowl (1 Fruit); pot of slime (2 Slime); scented flower or bottle of perfume (3 Flower); stable candle on a saucer & matches (4 Safety first).

## Activity

These four Mindfulness techniques could be built into each day for practise over time. They are intended to last a minute or two only.

Start each session by saying, 'Calm-Down Time', then ask for silence.

### 1 Fruit

Say: 'Take a piece of fruit from the bowl. Close your eyes. Eat the fruit very, very slowly, really noticing how it feels and tastes.'

Page 1 of 2

## 2 Slime

Say: 'Take a handful of slime. Close your eyes and play with it very slowly for a minute or so. Notice:

- What you feel
- What you hear
- What you smell

## 3 Flower

Model sniffing the flower/perfume bottle slowly, with your eyes shut. Then invite the children (one at a time, in a group) to close their eyes and sniff. Say: 'Sniff slowly, slowly.'

## 4 Safety first

Light the candle and model blowing it out slowly. Relight the candle and ask the children (one at a time, in a group) to blow it out slowly, just as you did.

# Activity 23
# What's in the Box?

☑ **Small groups**

## Aims

To learn cooperation and turn-taking.

## Materials

Large selection of items, mostly (but not all) toys: e.g., 'Small World' toys, model food, soft toys, toy cars, building blocks, dressing-up items (e.g., hard hat, wand). In addition to toys, have a few of the following or similar: books, household items (e.g., wooden spoon), shoe, hat. Put the items in a lidded box big enough to hold them: cut a hole in the lid for pulling out individual items. The box could be decorated and named by the children.

## Activity

A group of two to four children is needed, plus (ideally) two adults to model language and behaviour. The activity runs as follows:

- Sit around the box.
- The adults should play first, to model the activity. Use the phrase: 'What's in the box?' Look excited. Then say, 'My turn'.
- Put your hand in the box and feel what is inside. Grab something. Look puzzled and excited. Guess what it is, saying, 'It's … '; then take it out and say the name again.
- Now say, 'Your turn', and use eye contact with the other adult, moving the box towards them.
- Note: One of the adults should model picking something out that they cannot identify. They should say, 'Help! I don't know what it is!', then take it out for the group to help name it.
- Once both adults have modelled the game, they pass the game to a child, saying, 'Your turn; what's in the box?'

*Page 1 of 2*

- Praise children for following the rules – every single time they do – even if they make mistakes! You can say 'good sharing', or 'good turn-taking', or 'good cooperating'.
- If children do not pass on the box, adults should model for them, sticking to the 'My turn, your turn' script.

## Variations on the game

- Try other turn-taking and cooperation games with the same 'My turn, your turn' script, but using (for example) musical instruments, rolling a ball back and forth, 'marble run', 'dress the doll', 'make the dinner' (fill the box with real or play food and compile a meal as a team).
- Fill the box with toy animals and play 'make the animal noise': the 'chooser' puts a hand in the box and takes out one of the toy animals and then makes the appropriate animal noise. The others have to guess the animal.
- Get the children to fill the box as a team.
- Pick three items and make up a story
- Get the person with their hand in the box to give clues about what the item is to the group.

# Activity 24
# Using Grit

 Individuals  Small groups  Whole class

## Aims

To learn to develop 'grit' and personal determination through challenges.

## Materials

Determined by the challenges (see below).

## Activity

1 Decide on a challenge suitable for your group (or individual child) and model 'gritty' ways to deal with this challenge. Activities should be planned that are difficult, but not impossible. Ideally these are 'stepped' activities, rather than ones that you either can or cannot do. Some examples of activities that could be used:

- Tree-climbing
- Tower-building
- Gardening
- Making up a story
- Puzzles
- Running
- Tying shoelaces

2 Use 'gritty language', in other words, language that praises persistence and grittiness rather than an end result:

- You can't do it … yet!
- It was hard, but you kept going!
- You have stuck at it – well done!
- You showed good grit there!
- You were not afraid to have a go and get it wrong – well done!
- Well done – you tried lots of different ways to do it!
- You did not give up!
- Brilliant – you felt frustrated [upset/angry], but you sorted it out!
- Well done – you worked it out on your own!

3 Make sure you provide children with space and freedom to 'grow' their independence. Do not step in immediately when they find it hard. If need be, encourage them using language, rather than doing it for them.

## Extension

With older or more able children, try asking them to make up a story about a child (or themselves) demonstrating 'true grit'.

# Activity 25
# Fantasy Island

## Aims

This can be a useful activity to identify and celebrate to what is important and valuable for the child.

## Materials

Large sheets of paper, coloured pens/pencils or crayons; Worksheet 20, 'Fantasy Island Cards', laminated and cut out individually. Optional: video recorder, collage materials, magazine pictures, photographs.

## Activity

This works well with individual children, but may also be adapted for a group, perhaps as a longer project involving the building of a map or model of the fantasy island.

1 Draw an outline of an island with the child: have some fun with the coastline and details.

2 Work with the child to identify things or people that they would take to their fantasy island. Take some time and have some fun drawing and sticking this information on and around the island. The cards on Worksheet 20 could serve as prompts.

3 The final island can then be used as a discussion tool if the child is able to engage with this.

4 The adult and child could make a video explaining the island and watch it or edit it together.

The activity is very flexible: it may be carried out by drawing, writing, collecting pictures and photographs, collaging, and so on. Children who struggle to use language may prefer to sort different pictures into two piles: what they would take to their island and what they would not (they can't take everything!). A few ideas are provided in the form of the cards on Worksheet 20.

## Extension

Tell a story about what might happen on the island.

# Worksheet 20

# Fantasy Island Cards

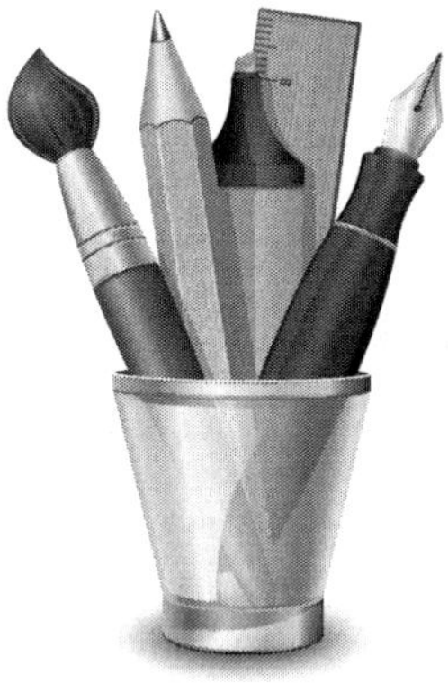

# Activity 26
# All about Me

 Individuals  Small groups  Whole class

## Aims

A useful 'getting to know you' activity that also helps to promote discussion within a group.

## Materials

A3 paper, coloured pens/pencils/felt-tip pens; magazine pictures, photographs, collage materials; Worksheet 21, 'Gingerbread Man' (one each, enlarged to A3 size). Optional: large sheets of paper (big enough to draw a child's silhouette).

## Activity

Tell the children that they are going to think about the things they like and the things they do not like. Ask them to draw a large silhouette of a person on a sheet of A3 paper, or use the enlarged Worksheet 21. Alternatively, ask a group to form pairs, with one partner drawing around the silhouette of the other. Cut this as it is not an issue.

The prompts below are useful in helping children think about what they like and dislike: you may wish to write them up on a whiteboard and read them out to stimulate reflection. Alternatively, this activity could also involve a thought storm in which you can ask the children to say themselves what they do and do not like. The children can then write or draw around their outline (either the Bear or their own outline) recording all this information about themselves.

Prompts could be:

- food
- favourite colour
- toys
- my best friend
- things I like
- places I like
- home
- school
- games & sports
- something I'm good at
- TV and films
- my best day
- people
- animals & pets

# Worksheet 21
## Gingerbread Man

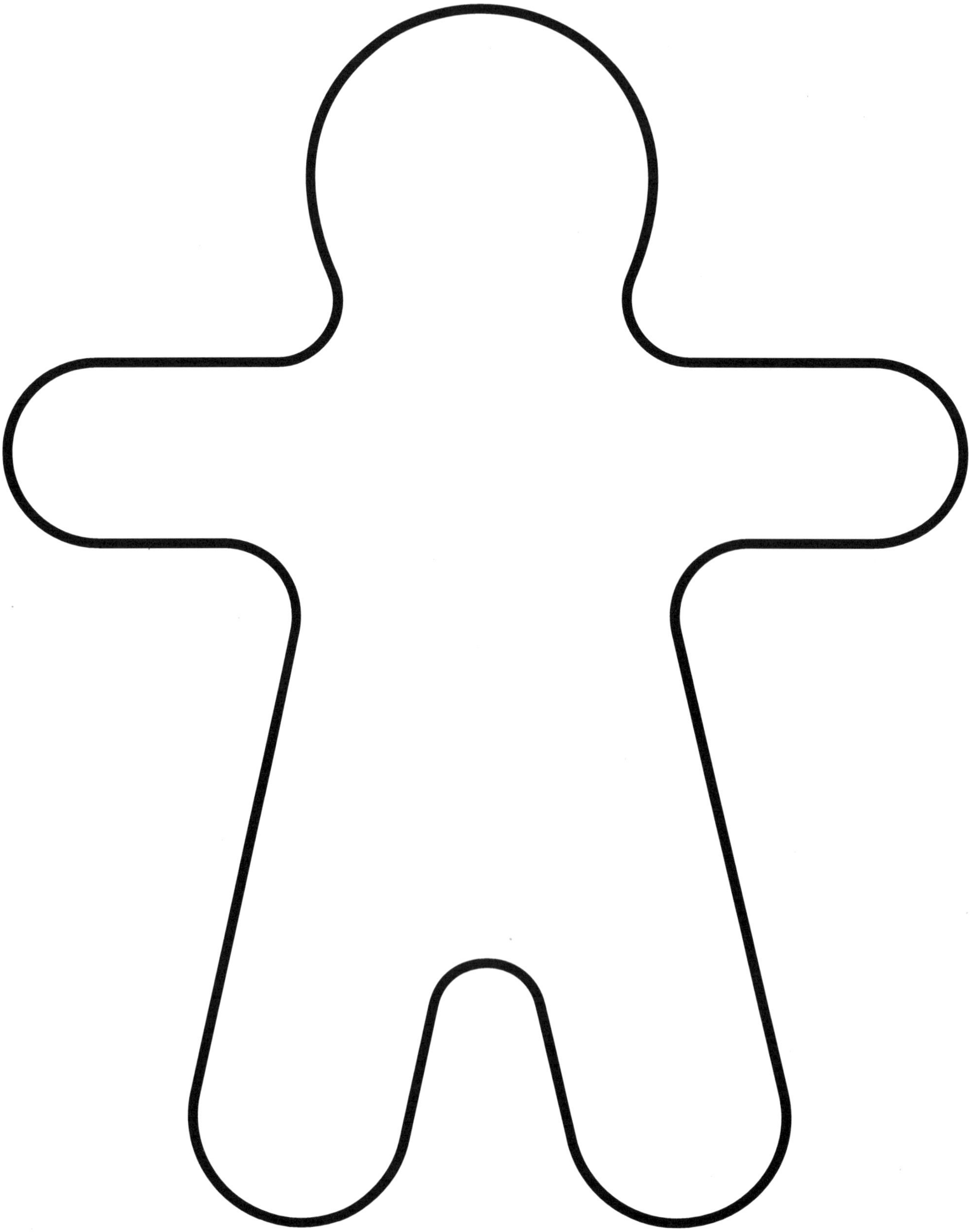

Worksheet 21

# Activity 27
# Bottling Thoughts

## Aims

To learn about how our thought processes work, and to focus on good, positive thoughts.

## Materials

Worksheet 22, 'Bottling Thoughts' (enlarged to an appropriate size), pen/pencil. Optional: magazine pictures that reflect a child's thoughts (allow the child to choose).

## Activity

This activity is only for those children who have some understanding that thought is a continual process that happens in your head, for example: 'that was fun'; 'I am scared'. Thoughts can be about oneself, about other people, or about the wider world. With young children, start by considering their thoughts about the world, for example: 'I love teddies'; 'Climbing is fun'. Help them to understand that thoughts are like talking to oneself.

Work with the child to help them notice and name positive thoughts, or even positive things they would *like* to think. Using the three bottles on Worksheet 22, write the thoughts and ideas down; you may choose to dedicate each bottle to a different kind of thought. If the child is very visual, pictures may be more appropriate than words to describe their thoughts.

Read out the thoughts, or refer to them periodically. The bottles can be put on the wall to remind the child of their positive thoughts.

*Page 1 of 2*

## Extension

If a child has lots of worries, this activity can be adapted to 'bottle up' the worries and take some control over them. Emphasise that 'bottling' their worries does not mean they ignore them; they are simply 'containing' the worries, so that they are easier to manage and conquer. Only do this with children who you know are worrying.

When you are considering worries, suggest that we can:

- Divide the worries into big worries, small worries and tiny worries;
- think about the places where worries happen;
- choose one worry at a time to work on;
- come up with one way to try beating a worry, for example: avoid it; confront it; say it out loud; laugh at the worry; cut out the worry from the worry bottle and throw it away; share the worry; make up a silly story about the worry; or 'think away' the worry.
- make use of a special 'worry time' – a time set aside for worrying. Together the facilitator and child 'get out' the bottled worries at the designated time and only worry about them at that time.

This activity can be adapted by using a real bottle, which is kept in a safe place.

# Worksheet 22
## Bottling Thoughts

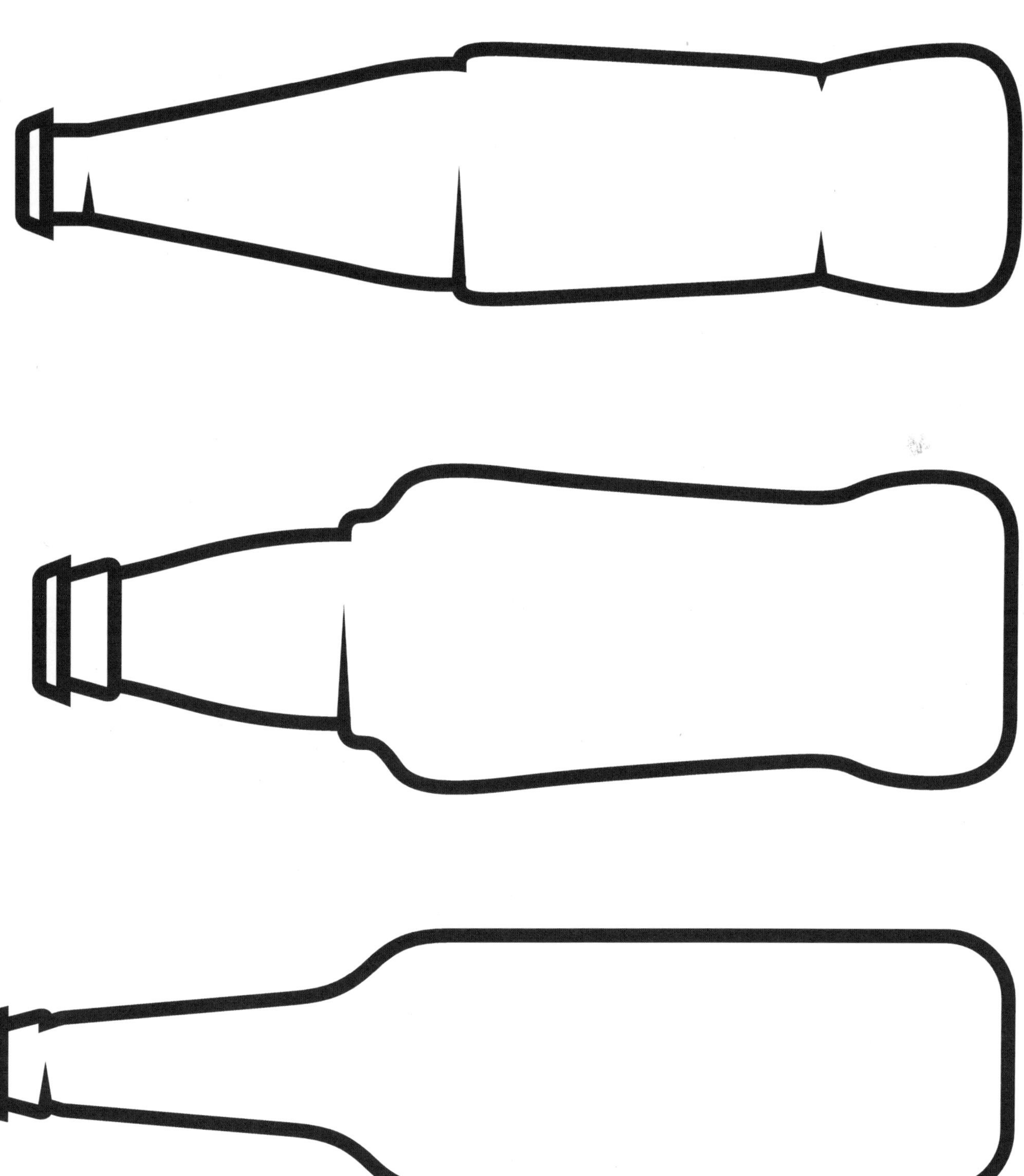

Worksheet 22

# Activity 28
# Helping Hand

☑ **Small groups** ☑ **Whole class**

## Aims

To reflect on personal strengths and supportive people in our lives.

## Materials

A4 paper, pencils/pens; a selection of magazines/photocopied pictures of people who are important to the children, scissors, glue. Optional: Worksheet 23 'Helping Hand' & Worksheet 24 'My Helping Hands' (enlarged to provide space for writing/illustrating).

## Activity

Each person draws around their own hand (palm up), or is helped to do so. Enlarge the hand on the photocopier so you have nice big hands! Older children may prefer to use the image on Worksheet 23.

Now ask the children to think about their own personal strengths and the people that support them in life. Then they could complete the worksheet as follows:

- On the thumb write the name of someone they trust and can talk to, or stick on a photograph of that person;
- On the small finger write or draw something that makes them happy, such as walking the dog, swimming, and so on.
- On the other fingers they could draw or stick on pictures of things they like;
- In the palm write something that they consider to be a personal strength, for example: climbing, building, being kind.

## Extension

- Ask the children to draw around both of their hands on separate sheets of paper and enlarge the images to provide plenty of space for writing/illustrating. Alternatively, use the image on Worksheet 24 and enlarge it.
- Together write the names or stick on the photographs of five people that they can go to when they need help (this could be someone they trust from home, a relative, a teacher or person at school, friends from school or friends from other places).
- They can use the second hand to write the names/paste on the photographs of five people they help.
- The facilitator might complete the activity too. Who do you talk to when you need help? And who talks to you?

# Worksheet 23
# Helping Hand

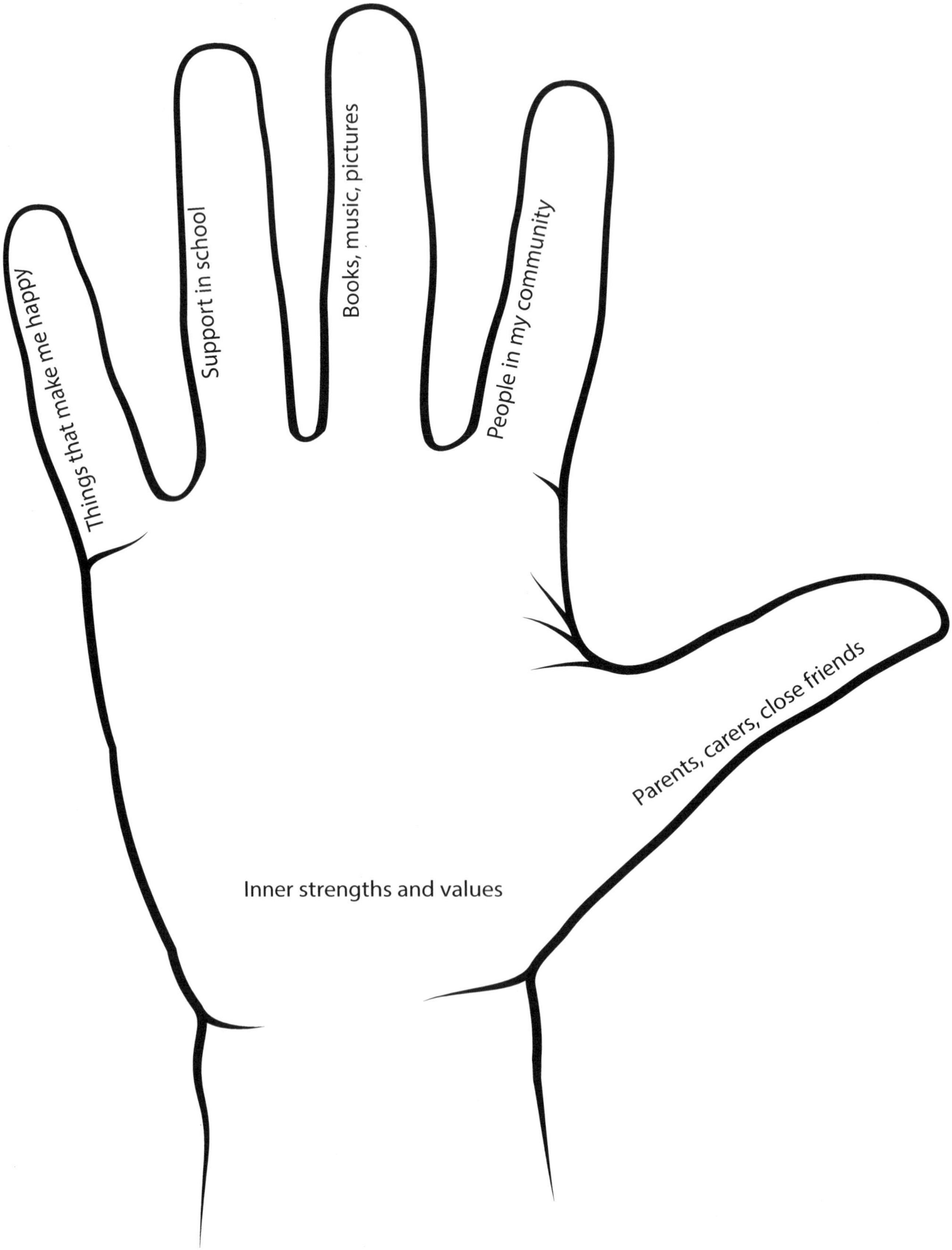

Things that make me happy

Support in school

Books, music, pictures

People in my community

Parents, carers, close friends

Inner strengths and values

# Worksheet 24
## My Helping Hands

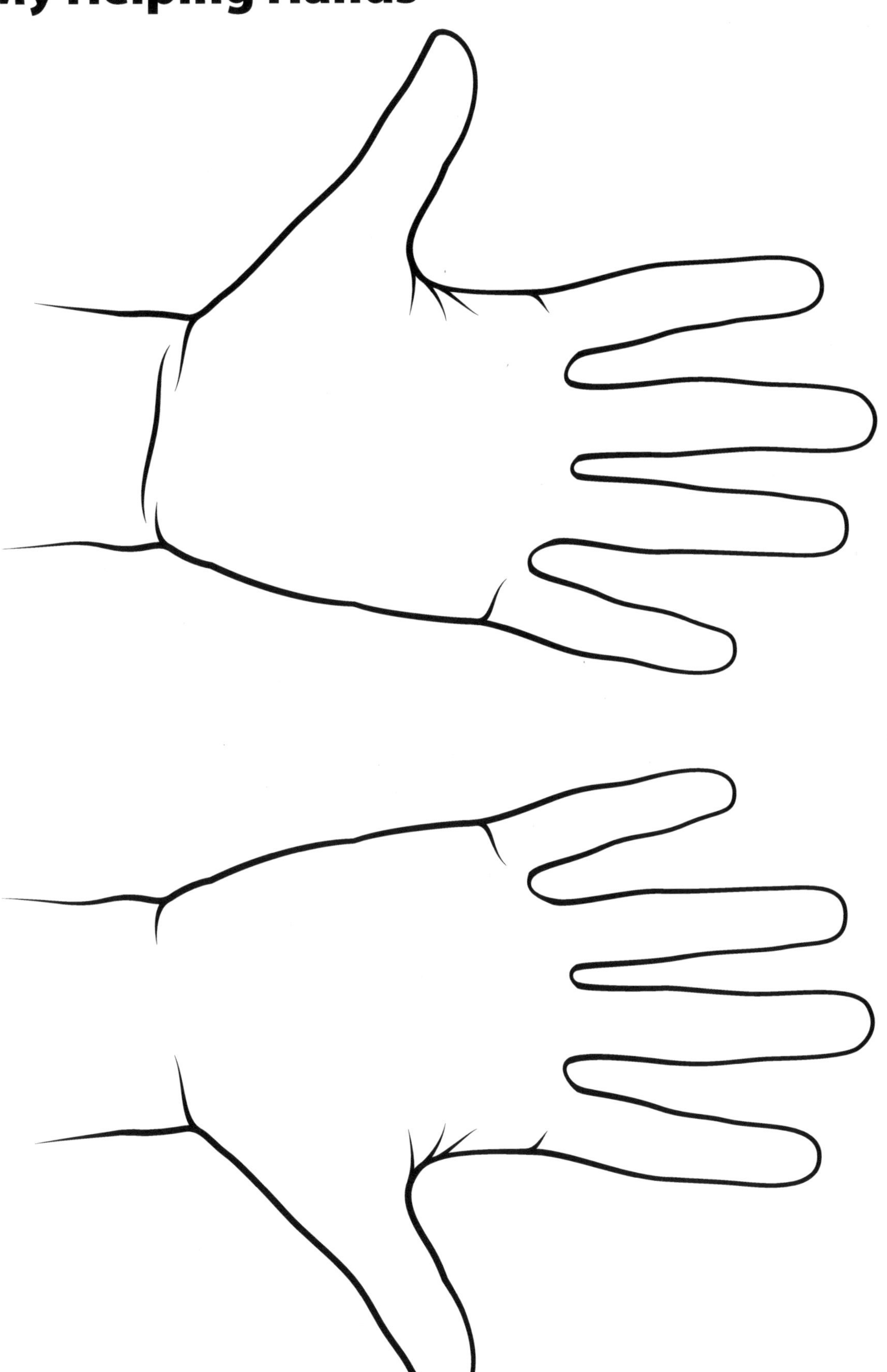

5 people I could seek help from:

5 people I could provide help to:

Activity Sheet 29

# Activity 29
# Problem-Solving

☑ **Individuals**

## Aims

To complete a task with the aid of a practical tool for problem-solving; increasing resilience and a sense that we always have choice, even in difficult situations.

## Materials

Worksheet 25, 'Problem-Solving Framework'; pens/pencils. Other materials, depending on tasks set: e.g., building blocks, cardboard & scissors, A5 paper & pencils, simple food (e.g., bread, cheese, chocolate), etc.

## Activity

Children who are resilient are able to solve problems on their own, or will know who to talk to for help solving problems. By helping children to develop feelings of mastery and control we are helping them to become more resilient and better equipped to cope with difficulties they may face.

Worksheet 25 is a problem-solving framework that we would hope the children will be able to use independently one day (not yet!). With young children we are seeking only to:

- Notice and name 'problems'
- Try out some different ways of solving a problem
- Be okay with trying out solutions that do not work

The focus is practical problem-solving, supported by an adult. The idea is that the adult models good problem-solving behaviours and praises the child when they demonstrate these themselves. The adult does not solve the problem for the child.

*Page 1 of 2*

Thus adult language and behaviour really matter. You are seeking to give the child as much independence as possible, and to highlight the times when the child is independent or managing failure, even in very small ways.

It does not really matter what the task is, but tasks must be 'solvable' in more than one way, they must be fun, and they must be challenging (but not impossible!). Here are a few ideas for tasks:

- Build a tower of [you decide number] blocks, which is [you decide height] tall.
- Build a bridge that joins that table to this table.
- Find a way to get at least one part of each person (facilitator and child) onto the 'safety' of a small piece of A5 paper, without touching the shark-infested waters all around
- Make a boat from things around the school or at home
- Make a simple jigsaw puzzle
- Make a sandwich with no kitchen equipment
- Make a chocolate heart.

If the child is very stuck, the adult may gently 'scaffold' them: 'scaffolding' involves supporting a child to problem-solve by voicing your own thoughts, for example: 'I wonder if we put that one there …'; 'I'm not sure how to do this, but let's try lots of different ways round …'; 'This might work better, because …' As soon as the child gets going again, the adult should 'step back'.

At the end of the task, celebrate and voice how you got there very simply, for example: 'We didn't give up'; 'We messed it up, but that was okay, we tried again'.

*Page 2 of 2*

# Worksheet 25

## Problem Solving Framework

What is the problem?

↓

List all the possible solutions– however weird or wonderful.

↓

What would happen if you chose each solution?

↓

Choose one solution and make a plan.

↓

Is the plan doable? How good is this plan? Rate 0–10

↓

Write down the outcome after trying the solution.

# Activity 30
# My Strengths & Skills

## Aims

To learn to acknowledge and celebrate personal strengths and skills.

## Materials

Worksheet 26, 'Strengths Cards' (laminated and cut out into individual cards) & Worksheet 27, 'My Strengths'. Optional: photographs of the child doing things they enjoy and are good at. Extension: Worksheet 28, 'Skills Cards' (laminated and cut out into individual cards) & Worksheet 29, 'My Skills & Things I'd Like to Do Better'; paper, coloured pens/pencils, pictures/photographs.

## Activity

For this activity you will need between three and five adults or children of more than 8-years-old, plus the target child. The target child must have good enough attention skills to listen for at least 2 minutes.

Spread out the Strengths Cards from Worksheet 26 on the floor and ask each adult or older child to browse the cards until they find one that they think is a key strength of the target child. Whilst this is going on, the target child can be engaged elsewhere, for example, in free play.

The child now needs to attend. Everyone can sit in a circle or in a relaxation area. One by one, each adult/older child picks up their chosen card, reads it aloud, says what it means and says why they picked it. For example, 'I think X is caring because he was kind to Y when he fell over'.

The child can now be helped to select their 'favourite' card, in other words, the one that they think is most like them, or that they are most proud of. The facilitator will need to support the child in their choice, attending closely to the target child's reactions and what they are saying.

*Page 1 of 2*

Using Worksheet 27, the facilitator can then support the child in deciding which strengths they have 'definitely, mostly, sometimes'. Celebrate the child's strengths by putting them up on the wall, perhaps decorated with photographs of the child.

## Extension

The Skills Cards on Worksheet 28 may be separately or in conjunction with the Strengths Cards in the same activity. After using the Skills Cards, ask the child to illustrate the skills that they are good at with pictures that say something about themselves. Using Worksheet 29, the child may then (with the facilitator's support) go on to list their personal skills, as well as the things they would like to be better at.

# Worksheet 26
## Strengths Cards

| | | |
|---|---|---|
| Courageous | Friendly | Responsible |
| Cautious | KIND | Supportive |
| FORGIVING | Honest | Warm |
| Talented | Hard-working | Courteous |
| Happy | Organised | CHEERFUL |
| Loving | Enthusiastic | Colourful |
| COOPERATIVE | Sporting | SENSITIVE |

Worksheet 26

| | | |
|---|---|---|
| Calm | Helpful | Reliable |
| Relaxed | Patient | OPEN |
| SENSIBLE | INDEPENDENT | Assertive |
| LOYAL | Fair | Positive |
| Resilient | Capable | Adaptable |
| Skilful | CREATIVE | Humorous |
| Powerful | Resourceful | Thoughtful |
| Caring | Efficient | Determined |
| Protective | Energetic | Adventurous |

# Worksheet 27
# My Strengths

## These are my strengths …

| Definitely | Mostly | Sometimes |
| --- | --- | --- |
| | | |

# Worksheet 28

## Skills Cards

| | | |
|---|---|---|
| Using a computer | Caring about other people | Dancing |
| Being generous | Having fun | Sorting out arguments |
| Keeping secrets | Sport | Jumping |
| Being trusted | COOKING | Singing |
| Saying 'thank you' | Speaking | Writing |
| Making people laugh | Being nice | DRAWING |
| Getting on with people | SAYING "SORRY" | SHARING |
| RUNNING | Helping | Swimming |
| Sleeping | Fixing things | Telling jokes |
| Working with animals | Listening | Being creative |

# Worksheet 29
# My Skills & Things I'd Like to Do Better

**I'm Good At …**

*Page 1 of 2*

One thing I'd like to be better at is ...

What Else?

Page 2 of 2

Worksheet 29

# Part 3
# Handouts for Parents, Carers & Professionals

1 Understanding Worries & Anxiety

2 Attachment

3 Emotional Literacy

4 Stress Busters & Relaxation

5 Building Authentic Self-Esteem

6 Motivation Matters

7 Using Emotion Coaching

8 Managing Anger & Tantrums

9 Problem-Solving

10 Friendship

11 Building Strengths & Skills

12 Offering Choices

13 Using Positive Language

14 Learning from Mistakes

# Introduction

Part 3 is a resource bank of informative handouts that can be used by anyone working with young children, including parents, carers and professionals. The handouts are intended to give practical overviews of key areas, with a focus on what we can do to support children within these areas, or to support adults who support children within these areas.

Professionals may like to share these handouts with other adults, as appropriate, for example by talking the issues through with parents, or using the handouts to structure workshops or training for staff.

The handouts are not a sequential 'programme' and are best thought of as a resource to dip into and out of, when required. The following are included in this section and are all photocopiable for ease of use:

1. Understanding Worries & Anxiety
2. Attachment
3. Emotional Literacy
4. Stress Busters & Relaxation
5. Building Authentic Self-Esteem
6. Motivation Matters
7. Using Emotion Coaching
8. Managing Anger & Tantrums
9. Problem-Solving
10. Friendship
11. Building Strengths & Skills
12. Offering Choices
13. Using Positive Language
14. Learning from Mistakes

# Handout 1
# Understanding Worries & Anxiety

## What is worry?

Worrying is something that all of us do, every day – children, young people and adults. It is a normal part of life. The stress that we all typically experience in conjunction with or as a direct result of worrying is something that we all need to be able to manage. It is particularly important for us, as adults, to be able to do this in an effective way as we need to be able to model such behaviours to the children we care for. This handout is designed for adults to gain a greater understanding of what worry and anxiety are, and to help them problem-solve around some of their own worries.

Even though worrying and stress is a normal part of everyday life, too much stress makes young people become anxious, exhausted, tired and unable to function appropriately. All of us have an optimum stress level which allows us to function effectively and efficiently in our daily lives - what is vital is that we learn how to recognise our own stress levels and develop coping strategies when we are experiencing higher levels of stress. This will enable us to maintain a healthy balance of tension, growth, rest and self-nurturing. We need to be able to focus and build up reactions that reduce stress alongside understanding, acknowledging and coping effectively with the sources of our individual stresses.

Anxiety is a normal response to a perceived threat, and includes physical, emotional and mental responses such as an increase in adrenalin, feelings of worry and confusion, and thoughts about danger and catastrophic outcomes. Normal levels of anxiety can assist people to be more focused and motivated, and to solve problems more efficiently. However, **chronic or high levels of anxiety** can reduce a person's capacity to respond appropriately or effectively to stressful situations or even normal routine activities. For example a highly anxious person may experience constant physical feelings of panic and may seek to avoid anything that might trigger their anxiety (such as being alone, going to work or talking in front of a group).

*Page 1 of 6*

Anxiety may be triggered in many different ways. Sources of anxiety may include (but are not limited to) fear of:

- Social situations
- Negative evaluation and rejection
- Performing in public
- A specific object or situation (e.g. storms or lightning/thunder, insects, blood)
- Separation from a parent/carer
- A parent/carer being harmed
- Harm to oneself
- Academic performance and exams
- Starting school or work
- The future (what will happen, how it might turn out)

Anxiety may manifest as a number of physical symptoms including muscle tension, shaking/ trembling and heart palpitations, sweating/ flushing or feeling very hot or cold amongst many others. In addition, children and young people experiencing anxiety may display a number of behavioural symptoms including withdrawing from friends and family, avoidance of particular situations and negative thoughts or pessimism.

When the anxiety starts to affect our general functioning, we may not just be feeling stressed - we may be suffering from an **anxiety disorder**. Anxiety disorders are considered serious mental health problems and are one of the most common types of mental health concerns for children and young people and adults. When the levels of anxiety are at this heightened level, it is clearly appropriate to obtain support via your GP.

## The Worry Cycle

We know that young children are not usually conscious of worrying and it is unhelpful to draw their attention to worry, or push them to manage it as an adult would. Our job as adults is to observe, listen and model resilience and emotion management. Part of this involves understanding our own worries and anxiety and managing our stress levels effectively.

Worry tends to manifest as a cavalcade of thoughts that come one after another, about events in the future or in the past. We begin with one worry and quickly build this into a series of worries.

This cycle can become difficult to disengage with unless we are able to challenge the initial worry and recognise that we have the means to change out thinking patterns.

Quite often *worry thoughts* start with things such as, 'If only I had …', or 'I must remember to …', or 'What if …', and spiral on from there. An example might be the thought: 'What if I have left the front door unlocked? A burglar might break in! Then all my things might be stolen … and then I'd have to go to the police … it would be terrible!'

Sometimes worrying can help us, by making us do things such as checking that we have locked the front door or completed a report correctly. But sometimes worrying can become a real problem when it actually prevents us from functioning effectively in our daily lives.

## Worry weigh-up

If you answer 'yes' to the following questions, then worrying might be a problem for you.

- Do you spend a lot of your time worrying?
- Does worrying get you really upset and anxious?
- Does worrying stop you getting a good sleep at night?
- Does worrying stop you enjoying yourself and getting on with things during the day, or at work?
- Do you feel that your worrying is 'out of control', or that once you start you just cannot stop?
- Do you feel worrying has affected your health (e.g., given you stomach aches, headaches, or diarrhoea)?

## What is anxiety & how can I beat it?

Worrying about things can make you anxious. Anxiety is easy to notice if you are on the look out for it. However, many people suffer from anxiety without realising what it is.

When you are anxious you may notice things such as:

- Heart rate speeding up, sweaty skin or going pale
- Feeling upset, on edge, angry, or irritable
- Feeling that something terrible is about to happen
- Throat or mouth dry

- Muscle aches or headaches
- Feeling tired, having little energy
- Poor digestion (e.g., stomach aches, bowel problems)
- Concentration problems (e.g., mind racing, inability to sleep)

Anxiety can make it more difficult to concentrate on work, to remember things, to get on with enjoying life. If you have a physical health condition or illness, it can also make this more difficult to cope with and even directly affect your health.

The more anxious you get, the more you worry and the more anxious you become! It can be a vicious circle.

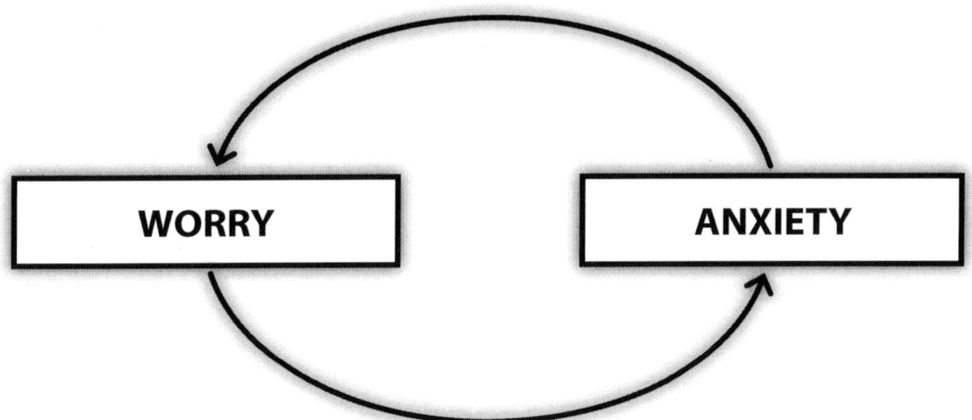


This is obviously why it is essential that we develop our own range of key tools and strategies in order to manage worries more effectively. The idea is to ensure prevention so that smaller everyday worries do not escalate into more significant anxiety issues or disorders.

## Basic ideas to manage worries

Here are some helpful tips on how to make worrying less of a problem and how to reduce anxiety which you may wish to share with your child or make use of yourself. Some worrying and anxiety are a normal part of life, so they will not go away all together – but they should not take over your life.

### 1 Notice

Notice when you are worrying or feeling anxious! This is the first step in making things better. If you feel the signs of anxiety mentioned earlier, or you notice you are thinking thoughts such as those listed earlier, then take note of these. You can even keep a diary or visual record.

*Page 4 of 6*

## 2 Stop!

When you notice you are worrying, say to yourself 'stop'!, and then see if you can get your brain to think about something else, especially something nice, relaxing, or enjoyable. Try doing something to keep your brain occupied (such as reading, watching TV, doing a hobby, or playing a sport).

## 3 Worry time

Think about your day and find a time in it when it would be okay to worry – no more than 5 or 10 minutes is needed. This is your special 'worry time'.

When you find yourself worrying at a time when you have other things to do (such as at bedtime, or while you are trying to concentrate on something else), tell yourself to stop and put off the worries for later, at your worry time.

## 4 Self-talk

If you find yourself worrying about the same thing over and over (e.g., 'I'll start my new job or course and no one will like me'), write down for yourself the opposite, 'positive' thought (e.g., 'People will like me. I'm a nice person'). Then every time you notice yourself worrying the first thought, tell yourself the positive thought. You can even write it down on a small card and carry it with you, in your pocket, to remind yourself of it.

## 5 Problem-solving

This is something you can try by yourself, or with another person. Remember – a problem shared is a problem halved! If you can tell someone else that you trust what your problem is, they can often help you with solving it, or coping with it. Try the following logical, problem-solving steps:

**Step 1**
If you find yourself worrying about a problem you are facing, write down what that problem is. Be specific – write down exactly what the problem is. 'I'm worried I won't cope', isn't specific, while 'I'm worried that I will forget people's names when I go to my new school', is specific.

**Step 2**
Then brainstorm all the possible ways you can think of to sort this problem out – even the silliest ones! Write them all down as you think of them.

**Step 3**
Once you have a list of possible solutions, go through them one at a time. Write down the pros (what is good about that solution) and the cons (what is bad about that solution). Think about the consequences of each solution: 'What will happen if I do that?'

**Step 4**
When you have all the pros and cons, decide which solution you will choose. If you can, check with someone else you trust whether they think this is a good solution. Then go and do it!

**Step 5**
Once you have done what you have decided, take a new look at the problem. Is it sorted out? Has it changed? Is it still there? Go back to Step 1 and problem-solve again if you need to.

## 6 Relaxation

Relaxation can be a really helpful way of making worrying less of a problem, and reducing anxiety.

- Get away from the things that are worrying or upsetting you – even if it is just for a minute. Go somewhere quiet (even the bathroom!), or just look out of a window for a bit.
- Breathing. Spend a minute thinking about breathing. Breathe in and out regularly and not too deeply, or too little. Sometimes it can help to count in your head while you breathe (for example, breathe in for three and then out for three).
- Relax your muscles. Stretch out your muscles and then let them go floppy and relaxed. This is easier if you have somewhere comfortable to sit. Make sure you include all your muscles, even those in your face, forehead, back and stomach.

# Handout 2
# Attachment

A resilient child will generally have, or have had, some experience of a consistent, positive parent or carer. They will generally be securely attached and will usually have an 'internal model' of their own being: worthwhile, safe and capable.

Positive parenting and positive role models (responsive, available, meeting the child's needs) can help to promote a person's ability to develop positive/secure attachment behaviour right through to early adulthood. However, we must remind ourselves that we cannot be positive and perfect all of the time and that is normal!

This handout is about understanding attachment behaviour and reflecting on some ways we might best support children who show insecure attachment behaviour.

## An overview of the psychology of attachment

John Bowlby came up with attachment theory, which included some of the following ideas:

- Attachments are a form of unique bond that all children make with significant adults.
- Attachment is about developing a style of attachment that is adaptive and useful to you in your local context.
- Children do not form only one attachment. There appear to be primary and secondary attachment figures.
- Although the first three years of life are thought to be a key time in attachment, attachment is a life-long process.
- There are many types of attachment and individual differences in how people respond to the behaviour they experience from caregivers.
- Through the 'attachment' the child learns an internal working model of: how people tend to behave; how emotions can be regulated; how likely it is that they will be given responsive attention; how much they are on their own, or 'in it with others'.

## Golden rules of attachment

Securely attached children tend to be:

- better learners
- more able to form new attachments
- able to ask for help easily
- willing to share adults' attention

Insecurely attached children:

- often feel lost and unnoticed
- may set out to reinforce their internal model (e.g., naughty, shy)
- may provoke hostile reactions in teachers, which reinforce their feelings of insecurity

What do insecurely attached children need?

- reliable adults who have time to respond
- predictable interactions and routines (or changes explained clearly)
- adults who respond to their needs (at the appropriate developmental level)
- clear boundaries
- specific attachment figures
- people prepared to challenge their negative internal models through sensitive interaction

There are many children and young people that demonstrate 'insecure' attachment behaviour. 'Avoidant' or 'ambivalent' behaviours are included in this category of insecure attachment behaviours.

Please note we are not labelling a child as 'secure', 'insecure', 'avoidant', or 'ambivalent', just their behaviour or 'behavioural style'. There is also evidence that the plasticity of the brain means that our 'styles' or 'internal working models' can change.

## What is 'avoidant' attachment behaviour?

It is a type of insecure attachment behaviour linked to having had consistently unavailable care.

### Approach to school & structure

- apparent indifference to uncertainty in new situations

### Response to adults

- denial of need of support
- sensitivity to proximity of adult

### Response to tasks

- seems to needs to be autonomous and independent
- hostility towards the adult may be directed towards the task
- the task operates as an emotional safety barrier between the child and the adult

### Possible skills & difficulties

- limited use of creativity
- likely to be under-achieving
- limited use of language
- may be resilient

In the context of school, the relationship dynamic within the avoidant behaviour profile can be summarised by the learning triangle (below), in which the child avoids the relationship with the teacher and directs their focus towards the task.

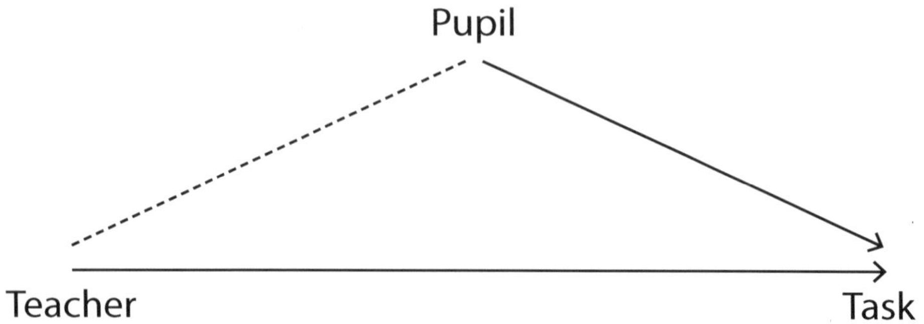


**Figure 4** Learning triangle for avoidant attachment behaviour

There are interventions that may support the child's development:

- The relationship between the pupil and the adult can be made 'safe' by the presence of the task. Highly structured games with clear rules and outcomes can assist in overcoming resistance to offers of help.
- The presence of another child can moderate the intensity of the adult's proximity. Pairs or small groups may help a child to experience closer proximity to the adult, moderated by the presence of others.
- Using another older child or mentor to act as an intermediary can be helpful. This strategy can enable the child to get involved more and defuse any tensions arising from the adult/student interaction.
- The learning/play task is the starting point for a child who finds relationships challenging. A well-structured task that may be completed independently can reduce the perceived threat of 'not knowing' something and feeling unsupported.
- Differentiation of the task, which acknowledges the child's need to exercise some choice, demonstrates that the pupil is being thought about and held in mind.
- Verbal expression can sometimes be inhibited within this group of children, so think of non-verbal ways to involve them and interact with them (e.g., through drawing, puppets and play).

## What is 'ambivalent' (or anxious) attachment behaviour?

It is a type of insecure attachment behaviour linked to having had inconsistent care.

### Approach to school & structure

- high level of anxiety and uncertainty

### Response to adults

- a need to hold on to the attention of the teacher
- apparent dependence on the teacher in order to engage in learning
- expressed hostility to the teacher when frustrated

## Response to the task

- difficulties attempting the task if unsupported
- unable to focus on the task for fear of losing the adult's attention

## Skills & difficulties

- likely to be under-achieving
- language may well be developed, but not consistent with levels of achievement
- may show resilience

The learning triangle for this pattern (below) reflects the child and adult at the expense of the task: interpreted in terms of early relationships, it may demonstrate an unresolved conflict, which does not permit 'another' to intrude into the parent/child link. In the learning situation, the child can be preoccupied with the relationship with the teacher, at the expense of the task.

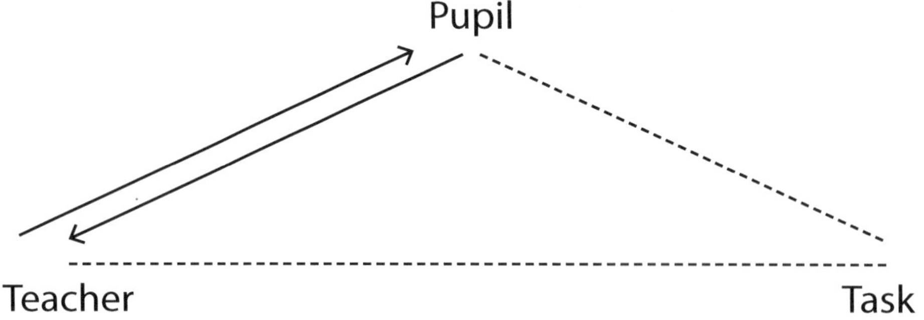


**Figure 5** Learning triangle for ambivalent attachment behaviour

There are interventions that may support the child's development:

- Differentiation of the task into small independent steps.
- Turn-taking to model the experience of two separate people working alongside each other.
- A timer can help moderate anxiety during short, timed, independent tasks.
- Board games provide separation and can also create opportunities to express hostility towards adults in a safe manner – with structure and rules.
- Holding a special (transitional) object can take the place of the adult for short periods: 'Please look after this for me for a while.'
- Making explicit comments across the classroom, or the use of eye contact, can be reassuring. They demonstrate that the adult is aware of the pupil and thinking about them.

*Page 5 of 8*





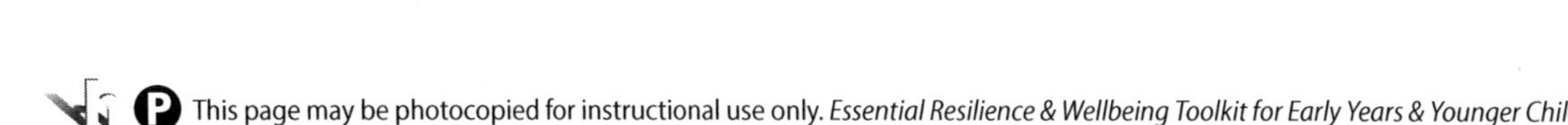

- Children with this attachment style may have a capacity to be tuned into others that will enable them to predict and control others in order to reassure themselves. This can be experienced by others as very bossy and controlling. For some children this capacity can become an asset in the classroom when appropriately directed into being helpful to the class in ways other than caring for others, for example, taking responsibility for a *task* rather than people. The children can then experience themselves as involved with others, as well as functioning with some degree of independence.
- Small group work, which facilitates peer relationships and provides opportunities to explore experience through stories of imaginary journeys, enables the child to experience anxiety safely, find support from peers and experience having a 'mind of their own'.
- Planning beginnings, separations and endings at the beginning and the end of the day can be helpful, for example, a planned withdrawal of the parent or a brief time in the office before going into class.
- Planning and warnings of changes and class movements can ease separation anxiety being triggered when changes take place.
- Reliable consistent adult support is important. The presence of someone to go to on arrival into school or care at the beginning of, or during, the day can assist a child with separation anxiety.

## What is 'disorganised' attachment behaviour?

This is a rare attachment style linked to the attachment figure having been, or continuing to be, the subject of the child's fear.

### Approach to school & structure

- intense anxiety, which may be expressed as controlling and omnipotent behaviour

### Response to adults

- great difficulty experiencing trust in authority of, for example, the teacher, but may submit to the authority of the head of the school
- may be unable to accept being taught and/or unable to 'permit' the teacher to know more than they do

## Response to the task

- the task may seem like a challenge to their fears of incompetence, triggering overwhelming feelings of humiliation, and ultimately rejection of the task
- difficulty accepting 'not knowing'
- may appear to be omnipotent and know everything already

## Skills & difficulties

- May seem unimaginative and uncreative, and find conceptual thought difficult
- Likely to be under-achieving and possibly at a very immature stage of learning

The triangular model for this pattern (below) demonstrates the difficulties in engaging with adults and with the learning task, and has long term implications for future adult relationships and access in society. The fear of many who work with these children is that there may be long term implications for mental health and offending.

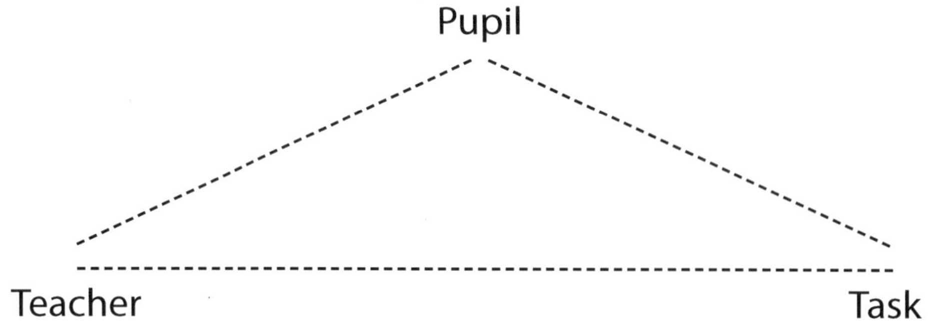


**Figure 6** Learning triangle for disorganised attachment behaviour

There are interventions that may support the child's development:

- Safety, reliability and predictability. The child's first experience of these may be to regularly attend a place (e.g., the school or a unit) where safety is assured and actively promoted by rules that focus on keeping people and things safe. School may be the first experience of a structured day with predictable activities and rituals.
- At the point of crisis (when fear is triggered) be calm, non-reactive and communicate some understanding. It is at this point that new pathways can begin to form, which provide alternative ways of responding other than fight–flight.
- Positive feedback can help to develop and reinforce more positive responses.

- Risk assessments are often imperative in order to protect adults as well as controlling reactivity for the child.
- Acknowledging the developmental stage rather than the chronological age is a useful starting point, since the child's learning may be at a primitive level. Repetitive tasks can be soothing to highly charged states, for example: colouring, sequencing objects/pictures, copying. Tasks should be obviously 'doable' and not need interpreting.
- It may be possible to explore feelings and situations without reference to the self, for example: via stories, role-play, puppets, drawing and play.
- In unpredictable situations that result in a sudden eruption of violence or distress, stepping back and engaging a 'safety routine', in which confrontation is avoided, is a good first step. For younger children this could be the removal to a safe, quiet and unstimulating place and or being given a box of routine activities.

# Handout 3
# Emotional Literacy

## What is emotional literacy?

Emotional literacy (often referred to as 'emotional intelligence') is our ability to recognise, understand and appropriately express our emotions. It is also the ability to recognise the emotions of others and to respond to them appropriately. Emotional literacy is a key component of both self-awareness and social awareness.

Emotional literacy is a key skill which encompasses:

- Self-awareness: being able to identify and recognise your emotions
- Self-management: being able to exert self-control and manage stress and challenge
- Social awareness: being aware of others' needs and having empathy for others
- Relationship skills: being able to communicate and relate well with others
- Responsible decision-making: being able to problem-solve and accept responsibility

## How can we help children develop emotional literacy?

We need to provide children with naturalistic and fun opportunities to:

- Learn to recognise and describe their emotions
- Learn to recognise and describe others' emotions
- Discuss and practise how to express their emotions appropriately
- Think about the consequences of expressing emotions inappropriately
- Reflect on their own emotional responses to a variety of situations
- Learn new ways to manage and regulate their emotions
- Practise effective communication skills and learn to moderate emotional responses when expressing needs, wants and opinions

## Two emotional literacy activities for children

Note: ensure you match the developmental level of the child to the activity. Remember that the main way we help children develop emotional literacy is by modelling it ourselves.

### Positive & negative emotions

- Ask the child to draw the outline of a body and write some 'feelings' words, or draw some 'feelings' pictures (positive and negative) around the outside.
- Encourage the child to talk about where in their body they might feel the different emotions and show this on the drawing, for example: 'nervous' could be sweaty palms; 'excited/afraid' could be tension in the tummy; 'pride' could be a big smile. This can help your child to recognise their stress signals and encourage them to talk with you about these.

### A rollercoaster of emotions

- In the course of a day we feel a range of emotions. The metaphor of the rollercoaster can be used to help children understand emotional intensity and the way experiences can lead to, or trigger positive and negative emotions.
- Draw a 'rollercoaster diagram' that shows the high and low points of a day. This helps children recognise events and situations that lead to varying emotional responses.
- Draw the rollercoaster that represents your own day and share it with the child, and then encourage them to try drawing one of their own.

# Handout 4
# Stress Busters & Relaxation

We know that stress and Anxiety disorders are an increasing problem for our children and young people and that we do need to therefore work more at a preventative level to support the development of key skills and strategies to manage such issues. Effective stress management and specifically using relaxation strategies can be very effective for many young children.

There are also some common sense ways in which you can assist children and young people to manage anxiety more effectively:

- **Support them to challenge underlying beliefs and thoughts** – Negative and irrational beliefs and thoughts such as, 'If I don't look perfect, no one will like me', or 'I can't cope with difficult or scary situations', are significant factors in generating anxiety. Model and communicate effective ways to question and challenge anxiety provoking thoughts and beliefs.
- **Support them to accept uncertainty** – Uncertainty is one thing that people worry about a lot because of the potential for negative outcomes. As it is impossible to completely eliminate uncertainty, you can assist children and young people to be more accepting of uncertainty and ambiguity.
- **Be a role model** – If you can manage your own anxiety, young people will see that it can be managed and incorporate your strategies into their own behaviours. Teaching parents to manage their own anxiety has been shown to be helpful in reducing their children's anxiety.
- **Be patient** – Sometimes the behaviours of anxious children and teens may seem unreasonable to others. It is important to remember that an anxious young person who cries or avoids situations is, in fact, responding instinctively to a perceived threat. Changing avoidant behaviours takes time and persistence.
- **Balance reassurance with new ideas** – When a child comes to you with something they are worried about, listen and understand what is happening. Explore with them what they could do to manage their fears.
- **Show children and young people some simple relaxation techniques** – Deep breathing, progressive muscle relaxation and meditation can be helpful as a way of learning how to better manage physical anxiety symptoms. Generally these techniques are only effective if practiced consistently over several weeks

*Page 1 of 7*

- **Encourage plenty of physical exercise and appropriate sleep** – When people are well-rested and relaxed, they will be in a better mental state to handle fears or worries.
- **Moderate the consumption of caffeine and high sugar products** – Caffeine products including cola and energy drinks increase levels of anxiety as they cause energy levels to spike and then crash. This leaves a person feeling drained and less able to deal with negative thoughts.
- **Make time for things that the child enjoys and finds relaxing** – These could be simple things like playing or listening to music, reading books or going for walks
- **Help them to face the things or situations they fear** – Learning to face their fears and reduce avoidance of feared objects and situations, is one of the most challenging parts of overcoming anxiety. Facing fears usually works best if it is undertaken gradually, a step at a time.
- **Encourage help-seeking when needed** – Make sure that children and young people know there are people who can help if they find that they can't handle a problem on their own. Knowing that they can call on others for support if needed will make them feel less anxious about what might happen in the future

## The importance of relaxation?

We all know that being relaxed is the opposite of being anxious. It is easy to know what the difference is if you notice what is going on inside your body and your mind at different times. However, this is often something that children need to be taught and shown. Using the two lists below can be helpful when you are supporting a child to initially distinguish between the 2 states. One shows what it can feel like to be anxious, while the other shows what it can feel like to be relaxed.

| Anxious | Relaxed |
|---|---|
| Cross, jumpy | Happy, calm |
| Heart beating fast | Heart beating slowly |
| Breathing fast | Breathing slow and easy |
| Skin pale or sweaty | Skin pink, not sweaty |
| Muscles trembling | Muscles relaxed |
| Stomach or headaches | No stomach or headaches |
| Thoughts racing | Thoughts normal |
| Can't concentrate | Can concentrate |
| Mind full of worries | Mind able to do what you want it to |

Handout 4

You can explain to the child that everyone feels anxious some of the time and relaxed at other times. If you were just about to take an exam, you would probably feel anxious. If you were getting ready to fall asleep, you'd probably feel relaxed. No one is relaxed all the time and usually there is a balance between the two. It is important to point out that sometimes that balance is wrong and you can find that you spend a lot of time feeling anxious and not enough time feeling relaxed.

If this balance is not right then naturally we will become unhappy and anxious. For a child this may result in them feeling tired, cross, sad, or as if they are unable to concentrate properly during the day. They may also experience bad dreams, or make it difficulty in sleeping. Sometimes it can give them headaches, stomach aches, or bowel problems. Often other people around them notice because the person may not seem their normal self (e.g., they may argue a lot, get into fights, or just seem unhappy).

Teaching a child basic relaxation and Mindfulness strategies can be very effective in decreasing the 'wrong' balance and helping the child to become more regulated and happier. You can try out a range of strategies until you find those that best work for the individual child.

## Exercise 1: Mindfulness

Mindfulness is about getting into a 'mind-ful state'. One of the simplest ways to do this is to simply sit down on a chair, close your eyes and begin to focus on your breathing. As you sit still, relaxed but also alert, you can then direct your attention to the sensation of each inhalation and exhalation, and also become aware of the feeling of air as it enters and then leaves your mouth or nostrils.

It is whilst doing this that other thoughts will enter into your mind. The idea is to become aware of such intrusions, noting each of these in turn without judgement and then simply letting them pass.

Mindfulness training has at least five broad beneficial effects:

- Increased sensory awareness
- Greater cognitive control
- Enhanced regulation of emotions
- Acceptance of transient thoughts and feelings
- The capacity to regulate attention

*Page 3 of 7*

Some other mindfulness exercises to try:

- Close your eyes. Breathe in slowly through the nose as if you are smelling a lovely flower. Breathe out slowly through the mouth as if you are blowing out a candle flame.
- Take a blank page and create an image of your favourite or most special place. Think about somewhere that you would choose to go to, to relax. This place can be imaginary or real, inside or outside. Make sure you fill your special place with all the things you would like to help you relax.
- Stretch your arms over your head, reaching for the sky; shrug your shoulders tight into your neck and curl up into a ball, as if you are a tortoise hiding in its shell; wrinkle your nose as if you are trying to get a bug off your nose; clench your jaw and then release; imagine it has been raining and you are standing barefoot in mud, then visualise yourself squishing your toes in the mud – wriggle your toes about in your shoes.
- Be aware of one pleasant event or occurrence each day while it is happening.
- Keep a gratitude or pleasant events diary.

## Effective coping strategies & calming self-talk

### What are coping strategies?

- Coping strategies are the thoughts, feelings and actions that we use to help deal with the challenges, stresses and demands we all face.
- They include the things we do to help us to calm down, cheer up, confront fears, deal with challenges, work at a problem, or to continue to work hard at something even when we do not feel like it.
- Some coping strategies are more productive than others, so we need to be able to use a range of effective coping strategies to help us deal well with life and its challenges.
- Children and young people tend to learn how to cope by copying the strategies that they see others use. They can also learn new strategies when provided with activities that assist them to reflect on what works and to try new techniques.
- Parents can help by modelling healthy coping strategies, and by talking with children and young people about the kinds of strategies they can use in different sorts of situations.

Handout 4

## Some coping strategies work better than others

Research highlights that while some coping strategies are helpful and effective, others are ineffective or even harmful.

| Ineffective Coping Strategies | Effective Coping Strategies |
|---|---|
| (Try to *minimise and model* use of these): | (Try to *maximise and model* use of these): |
| ❖ Worry | ❖ Work hard |
| ❖ Self-blame | ❖ Focus on solving the problem |
| ❖ Keep things to self | ❖ Seek relaxing diversions |
| ❖ Tension reduction (via alcohol, acting out, displays of anger and distress) | ❖ Seek physical recreation |

## Why model self-calming & coping strategies?

To help children start to:

- Identify emotions and feelings related to stress
- Recognise common stressors
- Reflect on personal stressors and coping behaviours
- Identify positive and negative coping strategies
- Learn about different coping strategies
- Practise a variety of positive strategies
- Decide which strategies to apply at different times and in different situations

## What is self-talk?

Self-talk is the voice inside our heads that tells us how we are doing. There are two main types of self-talk:

1 Negative self-talk includes thinking the worst and blaming oneself, exaggerating and focusing on what is wrong and ignoring what is right. It is pessimistic thinking.

*Page 5 of 7*

2 Positive self-talk includes being more realistic in thinking about the circumstances and one's own effort, being grateful for the positives, recognising personal strengths and being realistic about the level of responsibility. It is optimistic thinking.

Use of positive self-talk is associated with greater persistence in the face of challenge, whereas negative self-talk is associated with higher levels of distress, depression and anxiety. Those who use positive self-talk are more likely to succeed. Positive self-talk can be learnt or strengthened through practice.

## Activities for parents and carers

### Positive coping profiles

Draw up your own 'Positive Coping Profile'. Try to identify 20 positive coping strategies you use, with at least one strategy from each of the following five categories:

1. Energetic activity
2. Self-calming activity
3. Social activity
4. Shifting attention activity
5. Getting organised activity

Model some of your favourite coping strategies with the child.

### Identifying self-talk

- Imagine your child is about to start their first day at infant or primary school.
- What might their positive and negative self-talk be?
- What could they say to themselves to counter the negative self-talk?

Handout 4

## Managing stress

Thinking about our own sources of stress and coping strategies can help us to role-model coping for our children and young people:

- Make a list of some of the stresses and challenges you face (include stresses or challenges in the physical environment, relationships, events, fears, anxieties or thoughts that affect how you feel either physically or emotionally).
- Talk with a friend about how these stressors might be affected by time, or how they might change over time.
- Discuss which positive coping strategies help you to deal with one or two of these stressors.
- Brainstorm some additional coping strategies. Review the list and see if some are worth a try.

# Handout 5
# Building Authentic Self-Esteem

Self-esteem is something that is learnt – children are not born with negative thoughts about themselves, they are learnt through childhood experiences.

Parents have an important part to play in fostering self-esteem in their children, and other adults and carers can also make a big impact on how children and young people view themselves.

## Ways to encourage authentic self-esteem

- Use praise, not only when children have done well, but also when they have tried hard, and when they need support to try again. Being told that we are good at something makes us believe that we are, and encourages us to have another go. Even when something has not gone so well, being told that we tried hard, and finding small points that did go well can help in developing the resilience to cope with failure. We need a lot of praise before we can take in criticism without damaging our self-esteem.
- Give them lots of experiences. Having the chance to do lots of different things means children can learn what they are good at and what they enjoy, which helps to improve their self-esteem and develop an identity. Watching people play music on TV is nothing in comparison to watching a live band. By allowing children to have as many experiences as possible, we are enabling them to be more informed about the world, which helps to improve self-esteem by creating the confidence to try new things. Schools have an important part to play in this, through after school clubs, school trips and visiting performers and artists.
- Find the child's strengths. If a child can be helped to find their strengths, it can make a difference to how they view school, friends and themselves. The Strengths Cards and Skills Cards used in Activity 30 (Worksheets 26 & 28) can be used for this: think about putting up displays and lists of strengths and skills somewhere where the child and other people can see them. Update the lists when necessary.
- Help children to achieve. Sit down with children to discuss/draw/play around their plans and goals for the future. Try to make the goals specific and make sure they are the child's goals, not yours! Do not be afraid to add or remove things from the list, or to change the goals. We do not want children to feel as if they have to succeed or fail in achieving their goals, but rather encourage the idea that they have control over their own lives.

*Page 1 of 2*

- Think about the language you use. The language you use can affect how children feel about themselves. Rather than simply saying, 'You're really good', or, 'You're clever', be specific, for example: 'You can draw dogs really well'; or 'You're really good at riding a bike.' Do not use generalisations, such as, 'You never eat all your dinner', or, 'Your work is always messy'. These are rarely true and do not make children feel empowered to change. Try to be realistic in the expectations you have of children, saying things like, 'How would you feel if …', since children often do not know how they would feel. Do not use comparisons, such as, 'All your friends manage to get to school on time, why can't you?' Criticise the behaviour, not the child, for instance, 'I didn't like what you did', rather than, 'You're a naughty boy.' Try to put yourself on the child's side: 'We've got a problem here. What can we do?' This makes the child feel supported in changing their behaviour.

# Handout 6
# Motivation Matters

This handout is about working with children's motivation. A key distinction is between internal motivation (rewards come from inside you, e.g., you feel good) and external motivation (rewards come from outside you, e.g., money, a sticker). Internal motivation has been linked to good outcomes. Thus, as adults it is important to think about ways to help children to develop their intrinsic motivation, rather than just rewarding them when they do something that impresses us.

One key element of this is helping children to believe that they have some control over the world: that they can become 'self-determined' (motivated and independent).

Self Determination Theory (Ryan & Deci, 2002) provides a framework to help us understand how to do this. It is a theory of motivation that emphasises three 'innate psychological needs' that must be met for a person to be 'self-determined':

1. Competence/Mastery: feeling you can do things;
2. Relatedness: feeling connected to others;
3. Autonomy: feeling in control of what happens to you.

Helping children meet these needs, or develop these skills is an important adult care-giving role.

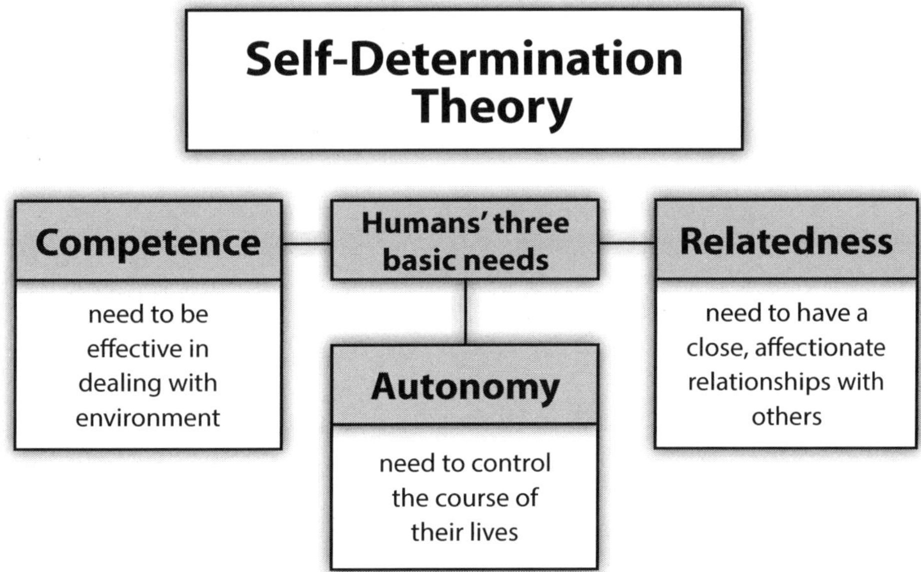


**Figure 7** Self-Determination Theory (Ryan & Deci, 2000)

*Page 1 of 2*

Ways we can help children develop internal motivation and self-determination:

- Model 'self-rewarding' behaviour, for example: 'It felt great when I did that!'
- Provide children with a range of opportunities to succeed.
- Help children notice when something they do makes a positive difference to someone or something.
- Build choice into activities.
- Ask for children's views and listen to their side of a story.
- When giving an external reward, try to give it for the process (the journey) of working towards an outcome, rather than the outcome itself.
- Give rewards after an achievement, rather than telling the child, 'If you achieve X, then I will reward you with Y.'
- Help children to notice and communicate what they are good at.
- Help children to notice when other people show independence, intrinsic motivation and self-determination.
- Help children notice the important people in their lives.
- Allow children to take some risks and support them to notice that they can cope with them.

# Handout 7
# Using Emotion Coaching

## What is emotion coaching?

Emotion coaching is helping children understand the different emotions they experience, why they occur, and how to handle them. In the simplest terms, we can coach our children about emotions by comforting, listening and understanding their thoughts and feelings, and helping them understand themselves. As we do this, our children will feel loved, supported, respected and valued. With this emotionally supportive foundation, the adult will be much more successful at setting limits and problem solving.

## Learning how to emotion coach

While emotion coaching may seem complicated at first, as we practise we find that it becomes second nature.

**Step 1**
Understand how *you* deal with feelings.

**Step 2**
Believe that your child's negative emotions are an opportunity for closeness and teaching.

**Step 3**
Listen with empathy and understanding, and then validate your child's feelings. Try to be an empathetic listener (Gottman *et al.*, 1996): use your eyes to identify physical evidence of your child's emotions; use your ears to hear the underlying messages behind what a child is saying; use your imagination to put yourself in the child's shoes; and use your words to reflect back what you hear, see and imagine in a soothing, non-judgmental way.

**Step 4**
Label your child's emotions. Keep in mind that it is easy to fall into the trap of telling your child how they *ought* to feel instead of *what* they are feeling!

*Page 1 of 2*

**Step 5**

Set limits, while exploring possible solutions to the problem that caused the negative emotion. John Gottman (1996) describes several parts to this step:

1. Set limits. Even though it is important to validate the child's feelings, we do not have to validate their actions. Once we set a limit on inappropriate behaviour and its consequences, we can follow through and be consistent.
2. Identify goals. Simply ask the child what they were trying to accomplish.
3. Think of possible solutions with the child.
4. Evaluate the proposed solutions together.
5. Help the child choose a solution.

# Handout 8
# Managing Anger & Tantrums

Young people – in fact, all human beings – need to be able to manage their anger effectively. The goal is not to repress or suppress anger as it is an entirely natural feeling with evident evolutionary and adaptive significance, but rather to express it effectively. When faced with anger we have two options available to us:

- Ineffective expression: irrational or hostile expressions of anger, such as violence
- Effective expression: to learn from past experiences and allow others to have their point of view

Clearly the main objective of any kind of intervention for children and young people who have difficulties in managing their anger is to encourage their ability to learn through self-reflection and experience, build their self-esteem and confidence levels so that they can allow others to have their point of view and respect and tolerate differences. The significant long-term effects of problem anger need to be discussed also including the detrimental effects on physical and mental health; problems in family life and friendships/relationships; difficulties in achieving and being successful in a school or learning context; and problems with the law, for example when young people 'lose it' and engage in aggression and violence towards others. Individuals struggling with anger tend to employ one of the following strategies:

- Displacement: Blaming another person or object for their negative feelings
- Repression: Containing thoughts in the subconscious
- Suppression: Hiding emotion for fear of disapproval of others

How an individual experiences anger will depend on the following:

- Learned response from parents
- Belief systems i.e. our thoughts and understanding of situations and ourselves
- Unconscious motivators such as fears, for example separation
- Individual differences i.e. genetic or biological differences

## Building resilience to manage anger

A resilient person who feels worried or under pressure will tend towards problem-solving behaviour, rather than avoidant or aggressive behaviour. In the early years children are learning this resilience, including how to manage feelings, especially anger. It is our role as adults to help them extend this resilience and begin managing their emotions with increasing independence.

However, it is important to remember that angry outbursts and tantrums are developmentally normal during the early years. Reasons for this include: impulsivity; developing communication skills; developing personalities. Our role is to understand the child's developmental level and thus appropriately support the development of their communication skills and emotion-regulation skills. This handout contains a few ideas regarding how to do this.

## Strategies for supporting the development of emotion regulation & communication skills

- Reflect on and name your feelings often and model problem-solving behaviour and emotion regulation, for example: 'I feel happy because ...'; 'I am confused.' Think about how you communicate these emotions, using your face, body language and tone of voice.
- Be attentive to and name the feelings of the child, checking your understanding with them, for example: 'I think you might feel ...?'; 'You are worried about the dog?'
- To develop vocabulary (including emotional vocabulary) read to and with children when you can.
- Notice distractions that work to move the child on from their tantrum.
- Use a calm voice even when you do not feel calm!
- Consider what the child's behaviour is communicating. Bear in mind that anger is often a secondary emotion, resulting from other emotions, for example, frustration. When we do not have the language to communicate, we use behaviour. Here are a few ideas to help you investigate the reasons behind children's behaviour:
    - Use an ABCC chart. This is a big table with columns for A (Antecedents: what came just before the behaviour); B (Behaviour); C (Consequences: what happened just after the behaviour); and C (Communication: what might the child have been communicating).
    - Consider common reasons for 'difficult' behaviour: a desire to obtain access to certain things, situations or people; an attempt to seek social contact; an attempt to escape; overstimulation.





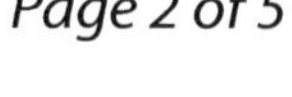

— Hypothesise. Once you have a hypothesis as to what the behaviour might be communicating, try it out by, for example, immediately supplying the desired object.

## Some key Anger Management Strategies

You may wish to also make use of some of the most useful and commonly used strategies with children and young people as follows:

### The traffic light system

This presents children with a means of identifying, analysing and subsequently deescalating strong feelings. It is a clear visual image of how strong feelings can be managed as follows:

- The red light indicates the stop and think stage in which the pupils identify the problem - what is the problem? How do I feel?
- The amber light represents the wait and plan stage – what should I do? Who can help me? What are the consequences?
- The green light represents the go stage – try your plan, go for it, reflect, evaluate.

Children people can make use of this traffic light system on a regular basis and evaluate how useful or otherwise. The traffic light strategy can be used as a visual reminder in the form of a book mark and presented in poster form in a range of contexts around the home or school.

### Change your thinking

Once children know what their triggers to anger are they can then begin to change how they think about them by creating a new script. It is useful to present opportunities for triggers to be identified and for children to then identify what they think and do as a result of these triggers. In true solution-focused fashion they can then proceed to think and articulate what they could do differently, how they could think differently, how they could respond differently in the future.

### Developing a script

Children can also develop their own personal calming down script in order to diffuse a situation when they find themselves becoming angry. This can be written down onto a small card and kept somewhere safe.

Handout 8

## Using 'I' messages

Children can formulate an 'I' message which can replace negative responses or statements. For example, if someone is attempting to pick a fight with them or if someone is doing something that is beginning to make them angry they can rehearse an 'I' statement such as "I would like you to stop that now because you are making me feel angry" or "I don't like what you are doing please stop it" etc.

## Using exercise

Running out your anger or engaging in some form of exercise is particularly helpful as it produces the feel good chemical endorphin alongside having a further positive pay off in terms of keeping you fit and reasonably well.

## Using the tension scale

Children can imagine a tension scale from 0-10 (10 being the most upset or angry that they could feel and 0 being the state when physiologically they are back to normal). They can then proceed through a series of steps: 1) I am upset because 2) I am at point ... on the scale 3) to get down to point... I need to ...... 4) to get down to point 0 I need to ..... 5) when I am on 0 I will feel ....

## Using a relaxation script

Children can be provided with an age appropriate relaxation script which they can practise on a regular basis. Tensing and releasing muscles in each part of their body in turn. This can either be read aloud to them or they can commit the script to memory. This can be something they use prior to entering a more stressful situation or subsequent to experiencing a real pressure on their ability to cope and manage their behaviours and angry feelings/responses effectively.

## Use of distraction

Adults in a situation can often help a child by distracting them to another activity if they can see that they are becoming angry or stressed by a situation or event. They can also make use of distraction for themselves recognising the trigger to anger and immediately distracting themselves from the situation by engaging in a more positive activity.

## Use of relocation or time out

Very often when things get really stressful children may wish to take time out. In the school context, children can be provided with time out cards or some other means of indicating to the member of staff that they need to take some time to themselves in order to calm down. For younger children, this time out would obviously need to be supervised.

As an introduction to this area, the book *A Volcano in My Tummy* (Whitehouse & Pudney, 1998) is recommended and is a very useful resource to use with children experiencing anger issues.

# Handout 9
# Problem-Solving

This is a useful skill for adults and children alike. By modelling it ourselves and praising it when we notice it in children, we help children develop these skills.

A framework to keep in mind:

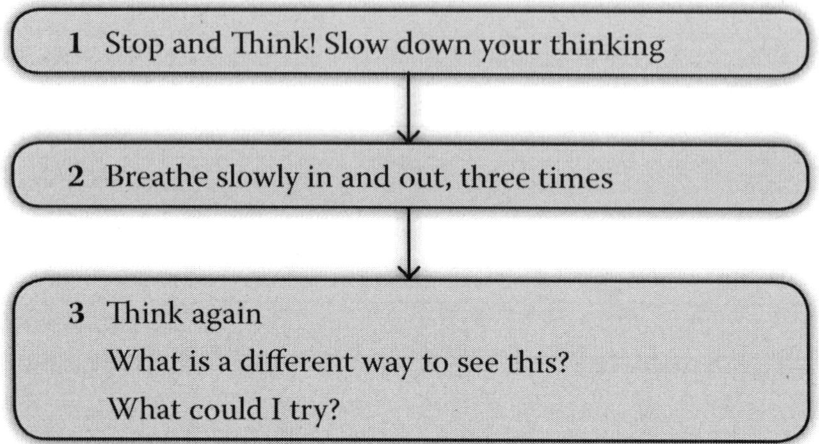


A few tips to encourage problem solving in children:

- Notice your thoughts and model noticing your thoughts, for example: 'I think that will work'; 'I wonder what will happen if I try it that way ...'
- Praise good thinking and problem-solving even if the child does not get a good result at the end or gets stuck.
- Play problem-solving and thinking games.
- Admit to getting it wrong and being okay about that!
- Notice good problem-solving in others (even if the end result is not perfect) and comment on it.
- Use puppets, rhymes, TV shows, and so on, to draw attention to problem-solving skills.
- Read stories together and discuss situations in which problem-solving occurs during the narrative.

# Handout 10
# Friendship

Humans are primed for social interaction and it is a key component of development. From about two months of age babies react differently to a child their own age compared to an adult. By 18 months they show preferences regarding peers they wish to play with. At 2- to 3-years-old most children imitate others and notice when others imitate them. Social hierarchies are developing and children are starting to develop reciprocal peer friendships.

It is through these social interactions that children learn vital emotional literacy skills such as turn-taking, use of language, conflict resolution, listening and cooperation. Our job as adults is to provide social opportunities and social support. We should also try to model good social interaction skills ourselves, such as listening to others, using social greetings, taking turns in conversation.

## Tips for supporting friendship skills

- Try to provide access to a range of peers and situations.
- Plan in structured activities as well as unstructured time. Children who find social interaction difficult often respond better to more structured games and play, for example, building club, or 'sing and rhyme'.
- Consider ways to encourage cooperation, communication and teamwork, for example, group challenges, or reward systems for the group rather than just the individual.
- Think about different roles that children play when interacting (e.g., observer, leader, listener, planner) and try to provide opportunities for them to develop different roles.
- Try subtly to monitor peer interactions rather than getting too involved (depending on the needs and context of the child and situation).
- Offer praise when children show good social interaction skills, for example: sharing, listening and not interrupting.

*Page 1 of 2*

- Observe children's social interaction skills to identify strengths and weaknesses and try to extend their skills in areas that they are finding challenging. One way to do this is via small groups or pair-work focused on developing key emotional literacy skills. It should be fun! Building, play, music, games and stories are a few ways to make it fun. Target skills could include: taking turns, saying hello, saying goodbye, listening, saying sorry, being kind, asking for help.
- Short, adult-monitored, activity-based playdates with structure (e.g., cooking activity, building activity, snack time, clear up time) can help children struggling in this area to grow their skills.
- Stories can be used to highlight key ideas about friendship, for example, sharing.

# Handout 11
# Building Strengths & Skills

Provide many different kinds of opportunity and encourage children to experience a wide variety of activities. Notice what children seem to enjoy and are interested in.

- Notice things that seem to feel good for the child and try to ensure that they are plentiful in the child's life, for example: water play, bath time, running, stories, dim lights, being with peers, animals, helping, and so on.
- If you can, include a short (e.g., 10 minutes) block of play entirely directed by the child each day. Have a box of toys just for this purpose and allow the child to lead, the adult copying the child and joining in. You could mark the start and end of the session with a bell or similar as you get out the box.
- Try some of the activities in Part 2 of this book.
- Try to find time each day to listen to, talk with, read with, and play with the child, even if it is only for short periods. Notice and support the child's preferred play.
- Give opportunities for a variety of play, including messy play, outdoor play, construction, imaginary play.
- Try to build in plenty of opportunities for independent, undirected play and praise independence, even if only tiny hints of it!

# Handout 12
# Offering Choices

Providing children with opportunities to choose activities and exercise their preferences can be important in developing their self-esteem and independence. Equally, we have a role as adults to help children develop an understanding of consequences, and this is best gained through real experience of the consequence of their choices. In time we link consequences to behavioural choices. However, remember that young children are seldom making real 'choices' with regard to their behaviour, as they lack the executive function skills reliably to do so.

## Ideas for offering choice

- As a general rule, limit choices when children are under 5-years-old. Most young children will struggle with a choice of over two options. A simple A or B choice is often the most helpful.
- If you (and they) are feeling robust, give some choices between two desired things, to help children cope with not getting everything they want; for example, ice cream or chocolate.
- It can also be helpful to give a choice when you would like a child to transition to a new activity.
- Praise children for exercising choice and for showing flexibility.
- Use visual methods and card sorts to support children to show their preferences and needs.
- Pick your battles: try to say 'yes' when children ask you if they can do something (unless there is a good reason not to), so that they learn that they have agency and that asking (rather than just doing!) is a good thing.
- Praise them when they accept a 'no' from you.
- Play some choice games, for example, closing the eyes and choosing something from a 'choice' bag.
- Try using 'First – Then' (or 'Now – Next'). The 'First' option is that desired by the adult (e.g., put your cars in the box). The 'Then' option is a reward or choice of rewards (e.g., tablet time, or 'choosing' time).
- Use visual supports when offering choices, for example: photographs, cards, or drawings.
- Make sure children get plenty of opportunities to engage in self-directed chosen play.

# Handout 13
# Using Positive Language

How we talk to children and the language we model to them (e.g., when talking to another adult or child) is important to children's communication development and wellbeing. What we say matters!

This handout contains a few ideas to provide language and language-building opportunities for children. Please do remember that none of us need to think about this all the time!

- Try using 'I' statements, for example: 'I feel …'; 'I need …'; 'I want …'
- Describe what you are doing.
- Describe what the child is doing.
- Describe how you feel. You do not need always to be certain, but can simply say (out loud): 'How do I feel, I wonder, now that …?'
- Describe your thoughts sometimes.
- Notice the kind of praise that you tend to use and the kind of praise that the child seems to like (e.g., public or private). Try to be specific in your praise and to praise actions as well as outcomes.
- Think about providing access to language in different contexts, for example, music and rhyme.
- Do not be afraid to use some words that children do not know yet. Accent them and include a simple explanation. Use them in a range of contexts. Repeat new words at the start or end of sentences.
- Reading and play are fantastic ways to develop language. Many positive outcomes are associated with children listening to 'expert' adult readers with whom they have a bond.
- Do not forget non-verbal communication!

# Handout 14
# Learning from Mistakes

## Frame 1

It is only a mistake if
you do not learn from it.

## Frame 2

I've missed more than 9000 shots in my career.

I've lost almost 300 games.

26 times, I've been trusted to take the game winning shot and missed.

I've failed over and over and over again in my life.

*And that's why I succeed.*

Michael Jordan

## Frame 3

James Dyson created 5126 failed prototypes of what would become his famous bagless vacuum cleaner before succeeding.

These are the attitudes we would like to encourage in our children! Making mistakes helps to develop our resilience, if we have the right mindset.

Page 1 of 2

## Supporting children to learn resilience through their mistakes

- Provide supported opportunities for healthy failure, for example: offer a difficult task (e.g., tying up shoelaces) and praise persistence with the task. Then structure the child gently towards success, for example: show them a video of shoelace-tying and get them to try again. Are they a little better? Why? Praise persistence and resilience. Ask children how they managed to improve – it has likely not happened by magic or luck, but by hard work.
- Provide plenty of opportunities to try new things, including difficult ones.
- Read and tell stories about characters who learn from failure.
- Model using feedback to inform what you do. For example, when you are trying something new, 'notice' (out loud) that you may not be able to do it yet, but that you are determined to keep trying.
- Model noticing your mistakes and apologising for them.
- Model taking responsibility for your actions and noticing consequences.
- Praise persistence and hard work over 'raw talent'.

# Part 4

# Recommended Reading & Resources

# Recommended Reading & Resources for Parents, Carers & Professionals

The following publications are relevant to the promotion of resilience and wellbeing in children and young people.

**Aumann K. & Hart A.**, 2009, *Helping Children with Complex Needs Bounce Back* Jessica Kingsley Publishing, London.

**Bocchino R.**, 1999, *Emotional Literacy: To be a different kind of smart*, Convin Press/Sage, Thousand Oaks, CA.

**Burton S. & Shotton G.**, 2004, 'Building Emotional Resilience', *Special Children* September/October 2004, pp18–20.

**Clifton D.O. & Anderson C.E.**, 2002, *Now Discover Your Strengths: How to develop your strengths and those of people like you*, Pocket Books, London.

**Craig C.**, 2007, *Creating Confidence: A handbook for professionals working with young people*, The Centre for Confidence & Well-being, Glasgow.

**Dean J.**, 2013, *Making Habits, Breaking Habits: How to make changes that stick,* OneWorld Publications, London.

**Duhigg C.**, 2012, *The Power of Habit: Why we do what we do and how to change*, Random House Books, London.

**Dweck C.S.**, 2006, *Mindset: The new psychology of success*, Ballantine Books, New York.

**Fox Eades J.**, 2008, *Celebrating Strengths: Building strengths based schools*, CAPP Press, Coventry.

**Frederickson B.**, 2009, *Positivity*, Crown Publishers, New York.

**Gerhardt S.**, 2004, *Why Love Matters: How affection shapes a baby's brain*, Routledge, London.

**Graves S. & Guicciardini D.**, 2013, *But What If? A book about feeling worried*, Franklin Watts, London.

**Green A.**, 2011, *Do Not Feed the Worry Bug*, Monsters in My Head LLC, Jersey City, NJ.

**Goleman D.**, 2007, *Social Intelligence: The new science of human relationships*, Arrow Books, London.

**Greenberg M.T. & Kusche C.A.**, 1993, *Promoting Social and Emotional Development in Deaf Children: The PATH programme*, University of California Press, Seattle.

**Hooker K.E. & Fodor I.E.**, 2008, 'Teaching Mindfulness to Children', *Gestalt Review* 12(1), pp75–91.

**Ironside L. & Ironside H.**, 2019, *Colour Away Your Worries: A calming colouring and drawing book*, Hinton House Publishers, Banbury.

**Jennings S.**, 2019, *Working with Attachment Difficulties in School-Aged Children: Practical and creative approaches*, Hinton House Publishers, Buckingham.

**Kabat-Zinn M. & Kabat-Zinn J.**, 1997, *Everyday Blessings: The inner work of Mindful parenting*, Hyperion, New York.

**Kaufman S.B.**, 2014, *Ungifted: Intelligence Redefined – The truth about talent, practice, creativity, and the many paths to greatness*, Basic Books, New York.

**Kraemer S.**, 1999, 'Promoting Resilience: Changing concepts of parenting and child care', *International Journal of Child and Family Welfare* 3, pp273-287.

**Linley A.**, 2008, *Average to A+: Realising strengths in yourself and others*, CAPP Press, Coventry.

**MacConville R.**, 2011, *Building Resilience: A skills based programme to support achievement in Young People*, Speechmark Publishing, Milton Keynes.

**MacConville R.M.**, 2009, *Teaching Happiness: A ten step curriculum for creating positive classrooms*, 'Teach to Inspire' series, Optimus Education, London.

**MacConville R.M. & Rae T.**, 2012, *Building Happiness, Resilience and Motivation in Adolescents: A positive psychology curriculum for well-being*, Jessica Kingsley Publishers, London.

**Naish S., Jeffries R. & Farrell A.**, 2016, *Charley Chatty & the Wiggly Worry Worm*, Jessica Kingsley Publishers, London.

**Nettle D.**, 2005, *Happiness: The science behind your smile*, Open University Press, Oxford.

**Pearce C.**, 2011, *A Short Introduction to Promoting Resilience in Children*, Jessica Kingsley Publishers, London.

**Peterson C. & Seligman M.**, 2004, *Character Strengths and Virtues: A handbook and Classification*, Oxford University Press, New York.

**Rae T.**, 2018, *The Bereavement Box: Supporting children through grief and loss in the Nurture Group*, Nurtureuk, London.

**Rae T.**, 2017, *60 Motivational Minutes Using Tools of Positive Psychology in the Nurture Group*, Nurture Group Network, London.

**Rae T.**, 2016, *60 Sensory Minutes Developing Sensory Skills in the Nurture Group*, Nurture Group Network, London.

**Rae T.**, 2016, *Building Positive Thinking Habits: Increasing self-confidence and resilience in young people through CBT*, Hinton House Publishers, Buckingham.

**Rae T.**, 2016, *Bouncing Back and Coping with Change: Building emotional and social resilience in young people aged 9–14*, Hinton House Publishers, Buckingham.

**Rae T.**, 2014, *60 Mindful Minutes: Developing mindful behaviour in the Nurture group*, Nurture Group Network, London.

**Rae T.**, 2013, *Purr-fect Skills: A social and emotional skills programme for 5–8 year olds*, 2nd edn, Nurture Group Network, London.

**Rae T.**, 2012, *The Anger Alphabet: Understanding anger – An emotional development programme for young children aged 5–12*, 2nd edn, Sage Publications, London.

**Rae T.**, 2007, *Dealing With Feeling*, 2nd edn, Sage Publishers, London.

**Rae T., Bunn H. &. Walshe J.**, 2019, *The Essential Guide to Using Positive Psychology with Children and Young People*, Hinton House Publishers, Banbury.

**Rae T. & Giles P.**, 2018, *The Essential Guide to Using Cognitive Behaviour Therapy (CBT) with Children and Young People*, Hinton House Publishers, Banbury.

**Rae T., Thomas M. & Walshe J.**, 2018, *The Essential Guide to using Solution-Focused Brief Therapy (SFBT) with Children and Young People*, Hinton House Publishers, Banbury.

**Rae T. & Such A.**, 2017, *Emotion Coaching: A resource bank for parents, carers and professionals*, Nurture Group Network, London.

**Rae T., Walshe J. & Wood J.**, 2017, *The Essential Guide to using Mindfulness with Young People*, Hinton House Publishers, Buckingham.

**Rae T. & Watson J.**, 2017, *Nurturing Social and Emotional Skills: A programme of work based on nurturing principles*, Nurture Group Network, London.

**Rae T. & Daly S.**, 2010, *Developing Social and Emotional Skills in the Early Years*, Optimus Publishers, London.

**Rae T. & Daly S.**, 2008, *Controlling Anger: A solution focused approach for children*, Optimus Publishers, London.

**Rinaldi W.**, 1992, *The Social Use of Language Programme*, NFER-Nelson, London.

**Seligman M.**, 2011, *Flourish: A new understanding of happiness and well-being and how to achieve them*, Nicholas Brearley Publishing, London.

**Seligman M.**, 2003, *Authentic Happiness: Using the new positive psychology to realize your potential for lasting fulfilment*, Free Press, New York.

**Schroeder A.**, 1996, *Socially Speaking*, LDA, Cambridge.

**Smith I.K.**, 2010, *Happy: Simple steps to get the most out of life*, St. Martin's Press, New York.

**Tough P.**, 2012, *How Children Succeed: Grit, curiosity, and the hidden power of character*, Houghton Mifflin Harcourt, Boston.

**Yeager J.M., Fisher S.W. & Shearon D.N.**, 2011, *Smart Strengths: Building character, resilience and relationships in youth*, Kravis Publishing, New York.

**Whitehouse E. & Pudney W.**, 1998, *A Volcano in My Tummy: Helping children to manage anger*, New Society Publishers, London.

# References

**Benard B.**, 1991, *Fostering Resiliency in Kids: Protective Factors in the Family, School and Community*, Far West Laboratory for Educational Research & Development, San Francisco. https://files.eric.ed.gov/fulltext/ED335781.pdf, last accessed 21/1/2019.

**Bowlby J.**, 1969, *Attachment and Loss*, vol. 1, Random House, New York.

**Bronfenbrenner U.**, 1979, *The Ecology of Human Development*, Harvard University Press, Cambridge, MA.

**Cameron R. & Maginn C.**, 2008, 'The Authentic Warmth Dimension of Professional Childcare', *British Journal of Social Work* 38 (6), pp1151–72.

**Cresswell C. & Willett L.**, 2007, *Overcoming your Child's Fears and Worries: A self-help guide using Cognitive Behavioural Techniques*, Constable & Robinson, London.

**Dweck C.S.**, 2007, 'The Perils and Promises of Praise', *Early Intervention at Every Age* 65 (2), pp34–39.

**Garmezy N.**, 1991, 'Resilience in Children's Adaptations to Life Events and Stressed Environments', *Pediatric Annals* 20 (9), pp459–66.

**Gottman J.M., Katz L.F. & Hooven C.**, 1996, 'Parental Meta-Emotion Philosophy and the Emotional Life of Families: Theoretical models and preliminary data', *Journal of Family Psychology 10* (3), pp243–68.

**Grotberg E.**, 1997, 'The International Resilience Project', John M. (ed.), *A Charge Against Society: The child's right to protection*, Jessica Kingsley, London.

**Henderson N.**, 1999, Preface, Henderson N., Benard B. & Sharp-Light N. (eds), *Resiliency in Action: Practical ideas for overcoming risks and building strengths in youth, families and communities*, Resiliency in Action Inc., San Diego, CA.

**Kabat-Zinn J.**, 1990, *Full Catastrophe Living: Using the wisdom of your body and mind to face stress, pain and illness*, Delacorte, New York.

**Masten A.S.**, 2007, 'Resilience in Developing Systems: Progress and promise as the fourth wave rises', *Development and Psychopathology* 19 (3), pp921–30.

**Masten A.S.**, 1999, 'Resilience Comes of Age: Reflections on the past and outlook for the next generation of research', Glantz M. D. & Johnson J. L. (eds), *Resilience and Development: Positive life adaptations*, Kluwer Academic/Plenum Press, New York.

**Perry B. & Hambrick E.**, 2008, 'The Neurosequential Model of Therapeutics', *Reclaiming Children and Youth* 17 (3), pp38-43.

**Roberts D.R.**, 2002, *Is this Self-Esteem and Early Learning?*, Sage, London.

**Robin A., Schneider M, & Dolnick M.**, 1976, 'The Turtle Technique: An extended case study of self-control in the classroom', *Psychology in the Schools* 13, pp449–53.

**Ryan R.M. & Deci E.L.**, 2002, 'Overview of Self-Determination Theory: An organismic dialectical perspective', Ryan R.M. & Deci E.L. (eds), *Handbook of Self-Determination Research*, The University of Rochester Press, Rochester, N.Y.

**Steiner C. & Perry P.**, 1997, *Achieving Emotional Literacy*, Bloomsbury, London.

**Whitehouse E. & Pudney W.**, 1998, *A Volcano in My Tummy: Helping children to manage anger*, New Society Publishers, London.